The Art of
PACESETTING
LEADERSHIP

DAVE WILLIAMS

The Art of
PACESETTING
LEADERSHIP

A Leadership And Ministry Development Course

The Art of Pacesetting Leadership

Second Printing 1999

ISBN   0-938020-10-2

Published by

DECAPOLIS PUBLISHING

BOOKS BY DAVE WILLIAMS

AIDS Plague
Beauty of Holiness
Christian Job Hunter's Handbook
Desires of Your Heart
Depression, Cave of Torment
Finding Your Ministry & Gifts
Genuine Prosperity, The Power To Get Wealth
Getting To Know Your Heavenly Father
Grand Finale Revival
Growing Up in Our Father's Family
How to Be a High Performance Believer
           in Low Octane Days
Laying On of Hands
Lonely in the Midst of a Crowd
The New Life ... The Start of Something Wonderful
La Nueva Vida (The New Life ... SPANISH)
Pacesetting Leadership
The Pastor's Pay
Patient Determination
Revival Power of Music
Remedy for Worry and Tension
Secret of Power With God
Seven Signposts on the Road to Spiritual Maturity
Slain in the Spirit — Real or Fake?
Somebody Out There Needs You
Success Principles From the Lips of Jesus
Supernatural Soulwinning
The Miracle Results of Fasting
Thirty-Six Minutes with the Pastor
Tongues and Interpretation
Understanding Spiritual Gifts
What To Do If You Miss The Rapture

Contents

Chapter 1

The Exciting World of Leadership

Some time ago, you made a decision to become a follower of Jesus Christ. Now, you have a desire to reach out and lead others into a fruitful relationship with God. That's terrific!

WELCOME TO THE EXCITING WORLD OF CHRISTIAN LEADERSHIP!

Your desire to reach out to lead others is an indication of a healthy personality. Look at what the writer to the Hebrews had to say about it:

For when for the time ye ought to be teachers, ye have Need that one teach you again which be the first principles of the oracles of God; and are become such as have need of milk, and not of strong meat. For every one that useth milk is unskillful in the word of righteousness: for he is a babe. But strong meat belongeth to them that are of full age, even those who by reason of use have their senses exercised to discern both good and evil.

– Hebrews 5:12-14

St. Paul, in his letter to Timothy, encouraged leadership. This is what he said about a person's desire to lead others:

> *This is a true saying, If a man desire the office of a bishop, he desireth a good work.*

> *—1 Timothy 3:1*

Paul showed us that it is not wrong to have a desire to lead others. In these Scriptures, he urges others to follow him, even as he followed Christ:

> *Wherefore I beseech you, be ye followers of me.*

> *— 1 Corinthians 4:16*

> *Be ye followers of me, even as I also am of Christ.*

> *— 1 Corinthians 11:1*

Don't let Satan cheat you out of your ministry with the false idea that having a desire to be a leader is selfish ambition. For years I struggled with this problem. I wanted to know that my desire for ministry was genuine: born out of a desire to serve Christ and His people, not self-manufactured. When the Lord showed me this Scripture, I knew what the difference was between selfish and unselfish leadership.

> *Delight thyself also in the Lord; and he shall give thee the desires of thine heart.*

> *— Psalms 37:4*

This is the key, if you have made Jesus Christ the delight of your life then the desire on your heart to be a Christian leader is not self-seeking, it comes from God. If your desire is to please Jesus, He will make you a leader as a natural overflow of your walk with Him.

Have you made the decision to become a Christian leader? Fantastic! This book is designed as a step-by-step guide to help you accomplish your goal. When you complete this book, the assignments, and Scripture meditations, ask your pastor to complete the certificate for you. This certificate will remind you of your commitment to Christ and His people.

Are you ready? Let's get started!

"Big jobs usually go to the men who prove their ability to outgrow small ones."

— *Ralph Waldo Emerson*

Chapter 2

Leaders Are Made, Not Born

For those of us who feel that we are not born leaders, this should give us great hope! When God created us, he equipped us with a fantastic amount of capacity and capability. He did not limit this for one person, or stunt it in another.

Leadership is a role. For example, I am a father of two beautiful children, but I was not born a father, any more than someone is born a leader. Fatherhood is a role I fulfill. I am also a pastor. I was not born a pastor. I just fulfill the role of a pastor.

Leadership is a role you fulfill when you lead other people. When you were born, the one who delivered you didn't say "Oh, my! It's a little leader!" or " Oh dear, a little non-leader was just born!" No, you were just a little boy or girl.

Instead, you become a leader one step at a time, as you take advantage of various opportunities to lead others. Now, as time goes on, God will give you more opportunities for leadership. That is *good news!* You do not have to be a "born leader" in order to be a *successful leader!*

Scripture Meditations

> Hebrews 5:12-14
>
> Joshua 1:8
>
> Matthew 16:24
>
> 1 Peter 5:1-3
>
> 2 Timothy 2:15
>
> Psalms 1:1-3

Thought Provokers

Can you think of at least three times where you were placed in a leadership position when you were growing up? List them:

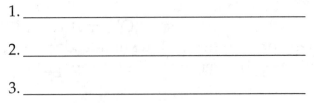

1. _____

2. _____

3. _____

Chapter 3

Requirements For Christian Leadership

Christian leadership has certain basic requirements. Since some people who try to be leaders lack some of these fundamental qualities on this list, they end up failing. We need to make sure that we lay a good foundation. Before a person becomes a Christian leader he should:

1. Be born again (2 Corinthians 5:17).

2. Be disciplined (1 Corinthians 9:27).

3. Be filled with the Holy Spirit (Acts 1:8, Acts 6:3).

4. Be joyful (Nehemiah 8:8).

5. Be filled with faith (Philippians 4:13).

6. Be in love with Jesus (Revelation 2:2-4).

7. Be willing to leave all, if necessary, to follow God's direction (Mark 10:28).

This is not an exhaustive list of the requirements of Christian leadership, but it consists of the major ones.

How could someone become a *good* leader in the church if he is not born again? How could he be a good leader if he is lazy, disobedient, has a nasty attitude, or is grumpy? This type of leader will be double minded, filled with doubt, love the world, or will be inflexible. People like this worm their way into leadership positions if a church is not careful. A leader like that can cause a lot of damage.

This is why leaders must be trained. A person who desires a position of leadership should spend a certain amount of time under the instruction of the pastor of the church. That way he will understand the heartbeat of the pastor. Problems are then able to be corrected before it is too late.

Scripture Meditations

John 3:1-8

Hebrews 11:1-40

Acts 10:44-48

Matthew 4:18-20

Philippians 3:1

John 21:15-17

Thought Provokers

Do you remember the time when you invited Jesus Christ to be your Lord and Master?

How do you know for sure you are filled with the Holy Spirit?

Are you willing to leave all, if necessary, to follow God's plan for your life?

*"The price of greatness
is responsibility."*

— *Winston Churchill*

Chapter 4

Make A Firm Commitment To Become A Master Level Leader

The word "leader" means very little by itself. For instance, a person could be a poor leader, a dictatorial leader, a lame duck leader, or a top-notch leader. We could go on, but I think you get the point. Anyone can call himself a "leader," but the kind and type of leader is what is important. I have found essentially three levels of leadership among Christians.

Superficial Leadership

This is leadership that is only on the surface. It is usually a title or position given hastily to someone who is not qualified or who does not really care about the job. For example, the boss makes his nephew into a department head only because he is re-

lated. In the church, perhaps it is someone who takes a job saying, "If nobody else wants the position, I guess I will do it." In the Bible, Ahab was such a leader: superficial.

Second Level Leadership

This kind of leadership is shallow, based upon some knowledge and some limited preparation for the position, but usually only enough to barely get by. This person is often the kind who has plenty of opinions and notions not based upon solid re-search, evidence or fact. He will often go off on tangents, find himself tangled up in error, and cause divisions because he does not take the time to thoroughly research his subject and do the job right. Second-level leaders, at best, achieve mediocre results.

Master Level Leadership

Master level leadership is a deep level of leadership based upon the pattern of our Lord Jesus Christ. Master level leadership is extra-mile leadership. This level of leadership is recruited, anointed and appointed by God Himself. Do you sense a tug toward some form of leadership? If you

do, begin to seek the Lord about it and start developing it.

In whatever capacity of leadership you serve, be determined to become a master level leader. Do not settle for second level leadership or superficial leadership.

What kind of leader are you? If God has given you an opportunity for leadership, are you willing to invest what it asks for you to become a *master level* leader? Will you settle for being superficial or second rate? I believe after you read this book, you will not want to be anything other than a master level leader.

Scripture Meditations

2 Samuel 23:2-3

Proverbs 22:29

John 7:16-18

1 Kings 3:1-14

Proverbs 29:2

Proverbs 12:24

Thought Provokers

Can you list some Bible characters, Old or New Testament, who fit into the three levels?

1. Superficial Level:

2. Second Level:

3. Master Level:

Now, go back and circle the level to which you are committed.

Chapter 5

Four Stages Master Level Leaders Experience

Every master level leader will go through four crucial stages, each stage building on the other:

Stage One— The anointing.

Stage Two— Preparation by study and prayer.

Stage Three— Preparation by practice.

Stage Four— The appointing.

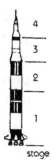

Each of these stages is essential to accomplish master level leadership. The appointing to ministry cannot take place without anointing, study, prayer, and practice. Many young Christians end up aborting their ministries too soon because they try to skip a stage or two and get ahead of God's timing. Here is a typical example:

Henry receives a "call" (an anointing) from God to preach the Gospel as an evangelist. Henry naturally assumes that the call is also the release for ministry, so he starts promoting himself to other churches, and perhaps even sets up some of his own "crusades." When there is little or no response, Henry feels that he is a failure and thinks that perhaps God did not call him after all.

Actually, all Henry needed was some more time in Stage Two and Stage Three. Then God would have released him to Stage Four and the genuine fruit of his ministry would have been obvious.

David was anointed as king over Israel several years before he was appointed as king. He went through a time of study and deep prayer and a time of practicing before he actually became king— his appointing. During that time, he endured a great deal of testing, hardship, and persecution at the hand of Saul.

Before Jesus left His Church in the hands of the remaining eleven disciples, He first called them, taught them, gave them practice, then finally. . .the appointing took place! They were then released for leadership and ministry.

Some mistakenly assume that because they have received a gift or anointing from God that they can jump right into leadership without any previous experience and become a success. However, before the appointing can take place, there must be a time of learning and practice. Otherwise, instead of an appointing, a *disappointing* is likely to take place.

My dad bought me a bicycle when I was a youngster. It was a free gift, just like God's anointing. Before I could ride the bicycle out into the street, I had to learn how the various mechanisms functioned — brakes, gear shift, lights, and so forth. Not only that, I had to learn Dad's rules for using my new gift.

Next, I had to practice on our property where Dad could watch me and monitor my progress prior to being "released" to ride in the street or across town.

The Bible teaches us that we are running in a race, and that we must press toward the mark of the high calling of God in Christ Jesus. There are no short cuts in the race. You cannot start midway or jump ahead to the finish line, or you will be disqualified.

Instead, start at Stage One, move to Stage Two, graduate to Stage Three, and when you are ready, launch out at Stage Four to become a master level leader!

Scripture Meditations

> 1 Corinthians 9:24-27
>
> Mark 6:12-13
>
> Luke 9:1-2
>
> Matthew 13:10-11
>
> Matthew 10:1
>
> Acts 13:1-4

Thought Provokers

Have you ever been on an airplane where the pilot was "anointed" to fly, but never had any schooling or practice?

Can you think of a time you launched into a project or a position before God "sent" you? What was the result?

Chapter 6

Qualities Exhibited In Master Level Leaders

Every master level leader displays the following basic qualities that are essential to leadership.

1. They have a faith filled attitude that says, "We can do it. All things are possible." According to *Harvard Business School Review*, a successful leader is 85% attitude and 15% aptitude. This is interesting in light of the fact that Jesus selected "ignorant and unlearned men" who possessed faith filled attitudes.

2. They have an unswerving sense of mission. Such leaders know that there is a God-breathed purpose behind what they are doing, and set out to accomplish their task for His glory.

3. They have a "get results" orientation to their ministry. Master level leaders lead people somewhere. They do not sit back and just manage a group or preside over the people, they lead them to a destination. They demand results, not just activity.

4. They have a desire and commitment to serve. This is one of the master keys to greatness. For example, have they become a member of the church? If they have taken on a job, have they committed themselves for a specific period of time?

5. They have an ability to delegate. The master level leader, like Jesus, releases the potential in others by delegating tasks and responsibilities. This also frees up the master level leader to invest more quality time on his own God-given priorities.

6. They have a commitment to quality and excellence. They take the time to do it right, not just do enough to get by. Quality means sorting out the bad from the good. For example, a good photographer is one who takes the time to focus and get the picture right in the beginning. If it does turn out bad, he crops it or destroys it. A poor photographer will show his poor workmanship. But, a master leader knows how to clean out the clutter.

7. They have a proprietary disposition. In other words, they act as if they own the place. If they work for a business, they take initiative and responsibility as if they own it. They treat everyone like a distinguished customer. They save the company money and constantly try to improve and expand the services of the business. Your ministry should be the same way: treat everything as if it is your property, and treat people as family.

Scripture Meditations

>Matthew 21:22
>
>John 15:8
>
>Acts 6:1-7
>
>Mark 9:23
>
>Luke 13:6-9
>
>Matthew 10:1
>
>Matthew 28:19-20
>
>1 Corinthians 9:24-26
>
>Acts 4: 13-31
>
>Luke 22:23-26
>
>Matthew 5:41

Thought Provokers

Can you think of a leader you know who possesses these seven qualities? Who?

In what ways can you develop these qualities in your life?

"You can have a dynamic life, but is necessary that you seize every opportunity to serve."

— *Mack R. Douglas*

Chapter 7

How To Develop A Servant's Heart

Jesus never rebuked anyone for the desire to be great. Instead, he taught people how to become great. The Kingdom way to greatness is this:

1. To become servant-hearted.

2. To become service-minded.

Greatness is measured by a person's willingness to serve others. Great restaurants know how to serve. Great gas stations offer the greatest service. Leading car dealers always give the best service to their customers. Great churches are more than just churches. . .they are ministries!

It's fun to look for better ways of serving. If you exercise the following principles as you work to serve God, you will experience ever higher levels of success and achievement.

1. Serve in a way that does not draw attention to yourself (Matthew 6:1-4). Some people make one hospital visit and broadcast it for six months thereafter. This is improper. We cannot expect fireworks to explode and the band to play every time we do a good deed.

2. Serve in a way that you can (Mark 14:8). Everyone is gifted differently. We cannot all serve as preachers or teachers, but we can all serve in some way.

3. Serve faithfully. Put your hand to some type of ministry (service), stick with it and God will put you in charge of much more. Your leadership will grow as you are faithful in serving.

Read in Matthew 25:21 what Jesus said about the servant who was faithful to his master and was a good steward of the talents given to him: "His master said to him well done, you upright (honorable, admirable) and faithful servant! You have been faithful and trustworthy over a little; I will put you in charge of much," (Amplified version).

If you serve others in the best way you can, you will guarantee your success as a leader. Jesus himself taught and exemplified this leadership principle.

Scripture Meditations

Matthew 20:26-28

John 15:15

Matthew 8:9

Matthew 23:11

Galatians 5:13

Mark 9:30

Romans 12:1

Thought Provokers

Give an example of something you are *not* gifted in doing.

What is one way you can serve others by using your talents and gifts?

List some ways you can improve your service this week.

"I make progress by having people around me who are smarter than I am — and listening to them. And I assume that everyone is smarter about something than I am."

— Henry J. Kaiser

Chapter 8

How To Develop A Teachable Attitude

A mark of wisdom on the part of master level leaders is the ability to remain teachable. It is impossible to become a master level leader without learning from other master level leaders. Here is a good saying: "When you're green, you grow. When you're ripe, you die!"

Stay "green." Keep learning and growing and don't ever become a "know-it-all." Nobody appreciates a person who thinks he knows it all and rambles on, telling others how much he knows. Make sure you learn from qualified advisors, not unsuccessful advisors. Usually it is the superficial and second level leaders who offer unsolicited advice. Seek out instead books and tapes by master level leaders. Learn from them. Stay open and teachable, all the while remaining attune to the Holy Spirit.

The wise man learns by listening. Poverty and shame come upon the person who refuses to be teachable. This being true, why do people develop an unteachable spirit, and miss their chance to have a lasting successful ministry? There are three possible reasons:

1. The feeling of self importance.

2. The resentment of authority.

3. The desire to do their "own thing."

He who is unteachable gets the "privilege" of learning things the hard way, through failure, embarrassment, pain or punishment. How much better it is to learn by listening to a master and avoiding problems altogether before they have a chance to happen!

Scripture Meditations

Proverbs 4:13

Proverbs 8:10

Ezra 7:10

John 7:17

Psalms 119:12

John 8:32

Acts 15:1,5

Proverbs 22:17-21

Proverbs 23:12

Thought Provokers

Can you think of a master level leader who may be willing to give you some advice? Who?

List some things you can do to make yourself more teachable.

"There are two ways of spreading light: to be the candle, or the mirror that reflects it."

— Edith Wharton

Chapter 9

Developing An Ever-increasing Desire To Draw Closer To Jesus

As a leader, you will need to tap a deep resource of wisdom. Frequently, you will face situations where there are two possible solutions, both which "seem right." In those times, you need to appropriate wisdom from the source — Jesus Christ.

In Proverbs 14 :2 the Bible says, "There is a way which seemeth right unto a man, but the end thereof are the ways of death." Oh, how we need the wisdom of Jesus to guide us through! As we draw closer to Him, we will find the solution to every situation.

Leaders receive a lot of flak from people. If you are a leader, you will receive criticism whether justified or not. Jesus will help you distinguish between constructive or petty criticism. This helps you to concentrate on what really is important, and keeps you from wasting your time chasing after little problems.

One week I received two letters from unsatisfied individuals: Letter "A" said, "We need to shorten the song service. It's too long. We need more preaching." Letter "B" said, "The song service is too short. We should lengthen it. We need more praise and worship." What do you do when you have two opposing opinions? Jesus knows, and if you seek Him, He will show you the solution.

As you invest time in prayer, you will begin to desire even more prayer time. The more you learn about Jesus, your desire to draw closer to Him will intensify. This is a key to genuine leadership success.

Scripture Meditations

Colossians 2:3

James 1:5-8

John 15:5

Matthew 11:28-30

Isaiah 10:27

Philippians 4:13

Thought Provokers

Have you committed a certain portion of your day to prayer and study?

Write a list of some ways you can draw closer to Jesus.

"Managers are people
who do things right, and
leaders are people who do
the right things."

— Warren G. Bennis

Chapter 10

Make A Firm Commitment To Be Authentic

Except the Lord build the house, they labor in vain that build it; except the Lord keep the city, the watchman waketh but in vain.

− Psalms 127:1

A ministry will either be authentic or synthetic. An authentic ministry is God-breathed and controlled with a supernatural flow of the Holy Spirit. Synthetic ministry is man-made and will be hyped up, pumped up, and kept alive by the natural energies of the flesh. On the surface, a synthetic ministry may look authentic. It is like plastic flowers or plastic fruit, it is not real. Authentic ministry grows out of a deep personal relationship with God, and moves by the direction of the Holy Spirit. Synthetic ministry is driven by selfish ambition and desire.

The Bible illustrates this difference in the lives of Ishmael and Isaac. Ishmael's life was synthetic; Isaac was authentic. The man-made persecuted the God-made (Galatians 4:29). Ishmael is a type of those who live after the flesh (man-made). Isaac is a type of those who minister after the Spirit of God.

Are you a "self-made" man? Did you build "your own" ministry or did God build it? Which type of leadership and ministry do you want to have? Authentic or Synthetic?

Scripture Meditations

> Galatians 4:22-31
>
> Titus 1:5-9
>
> Matthew 7:15-20
>
> Acts 20:28-31
>
> Matthew 12:33
>
> 2 Peter 2:1-22

Thought Provokers

Can you list a couple of other illustrative comparisons between authentic and synthetic ministry? Example: Real fruit verses plastic fruit.

What can you do to insure that your ministry is authentic, starting now?

"The house shows the owner."

— *George Herbert, 1651*

Chapter 11

How To Produce Fruit In Your Ministry That Will Glorify God

If ye abide in me, and my words abide in you, ye shall ask what ye will, and it shall be done unto you. Herein is my Father glorified, that ye bear much fruit; so shall ye be my disciples.

—John 15:7-8

Authentic ministry produces good fruit and reproduces itself. We reproduce *not* what we teach, but what we are. A plastic tree cannot produce real fruit. A wolf dressed in a sheep's costume can talk sheep talk, look like a sheep... but cannot give birth to a sheep!

An apple tree does not bear bananas! A counterfeit printing press cannot produce real money! God's first command to man right after the creation was to "be fruitful."

> *And God blessed them, and God said unto them, Be fruit-*
> *ful, and multiply, and replensih the earth, and subdue it: and*
> *have dominion over the fish of the sea, and over the fowl of the*
> *air, and over every living thing that moveth upon the earth.*

— Genesis 1:28

Jesus told us that our Heavenly Father receives glory when we bear much fruit.

> *If ye abide in me, and my words abide in you, ye shall ask*
> *what ye will, and it shall be done unto you.*

> *Herein is my Father glorified, that ye bear much fruit; so*
> *shall ye be my disciples.*

— John 15: 7, 8

But, how do we bear fruit?

We must begin with a seed. Everything in the Kingdom of God starts out as a seed. Even Jesus Himself was a "seed" that had to die in order to be resurrected and go on to produce and reproduce millions of Christians (good fruit). The first step to fruit bearing is to become a planted seed; die to your own self-efforts, self-dreams, self-ambitions, and then watch God work through you!

> *Verily, verily, I say unto you, Except a kernel of wheat fall*
> *into the ground and die, it abideth alone: but if it die, it bringeth*
> *forth much fruit.*

— John 12:24

Growth and production under Kingdom law always involve "death" first. My own ministry skyrocketed to success shortly after I gave up all my own ministry ambitions and told my pastor that I was available to help make his dreams come true. I laid aside my own personal ministry dreams, planted them as seeds, and went to work on making another man's dreams come true.

Soon my ministry grew, blossomed, and began bearing more fruit than I ever imagined. I found that I had to "plant" my dreams and "die" to them before God could resurrect them and turn them into realities.

Today, we worship in a beautiful 3,000 seat church. It's a reality! Before that dream could bear genuine fruit for the Kingdom of God, it had to be planted as a seed and die in my own heart.

Trees that bear fruit start out as a little seed created by God. Trees that appear suddenly have plastic fruit, and are man-made. Artificial trees cannot reproduce themselves, nor can they feed anyone. Which would you rather be?

Scripture Meditations

> Genesis 1:28
>
> Psalms 1:1-3
>
> John 15:7
>
> Revelation 4:11
>
> Matthew 13:31
>
> John 12:24

Thought Provokers

Can you think of some ambition, project, or program you are hanging onto, even though you never sought God seriously about it?

Is there anything right now the Holy Spirit is revealing to you that you must "plant" and die to in order for God to resurrect it into a supernatural fruitful ministry?

Chapter 12

How To Avoid "Strangulation"

Once you resolve to develop an authentic ministry and growth begins to occur, you must make sure that the growth is not strangled.

A goldfish placed in a small bowl of water will adapt his growth to the environment and stay very small. If you put him in a large pond, however, he will grow to be several pounds. If you place a growing pumpkin inside a quart jar, it will grow only to the size of the jar. It will be stunted — strangled!

Likewise, a growing church that reaches 80% of its capacity should start building or add another service to prevent the same thing from occurring

A growing pumpkin placed in a jar will grow no larger than the jar.

55

— strangulation! If the situation is left alone without serious attention paid to it, it will shortly reach the level-off point and begin to die.

A business also can encounter the same problem. If there is not enough manpower or capacity to handle the work load, the business will not be able to take care of its customers, and it will eventually level off and die.

Strangulation, according to church growth expert, Peter Wagner, can occur in three basic areas of a church: Worship space (sanctuary); Educational space (classrooms); and Parking space.

Concerning parking, there should be one paved parking space for every two church seats. In other words, if your church seats 2,000, you need 1,000 parking spaces. This assures surplus parking and prevents strangulation from occurring in this area.

I know a pastor who put in an additional 200 parking spaces and his church grew by over 600 shortly afterward. It was a miracle!

Avoiding strangulation is a practical principle to remember. This rule is true for businesses, evangelistic ministries, financial matters, and personal spiritual growth. You must strive to keep growing in these three general areas: Quantity, Quality, and Service.

Remember, Jesus likened the Kingdom of God to a mustard seed that grows and grows and *grows*

(Matthew 13:31-32). We must continue to grow, develop, and expand; otherwise we will level off and then finally die!

This does not contradict what I said about letting your *own* ambitions die. Self-ambition must die in order for God to resurrect it into a genuine, authentic God-given vision and ministry. Do not let the authentic ministry level off and die. Keep growing! Keep learning! Keep expanding!

Scripture Meditations

Matthew 13:31-32

1 Peter 2:2

Mark 4:30-32

Isaiah 54:2

Luke 13:18-21

John 3:6

Ephesians 2:21

Acts 6:1-7

Acts 16:5

Ephesians 4:15-16

Thought Provokers

Do you know any area of your life (spiritual, social, education, business, financial, family, or ministry), where strangulation is affecting its growth?

What can you do to eliminate strangulation in this area?

Chapter 13

Look To Jesus Christ And His Word As Your True Source Of Growth

Except the Lord build the house, they labor in vain that build it: except the Lord keep the city, the watchman waketh but in vain.

– Psalms 127:1

When a plant grows, it must depend upon water, sunlight and the nutrients from the ground. All of these are provided by God Himself. Jesus Christ is our Source of growth. We provide the seed and environment for growth; *He* provides the growth.

Do you want your ministry built by human plans, or by the plan of God through prayer? What kind of ministry do you want to build; a Kingdom ministry, or a personal empire?

True success, the kind that brings eternal results and eternal fruit, happens only when Jesus Christ is honored as the source of true growth. Do you want your family to grow closer together? Honor Jesus Christ as your source of growth.

A computer does not work very well if it is not plugged in. Similarly, we must remain tapped into the power source of Jesus Christ. Through His Word, we receive proper programming instructions that cause our ministry to grow.

We sow seeds for our ministry through preparation. Starting with a call from God, which is His gentle nudging in a certain direction, we can begin preparing for that calling. If we are not ready for growth, Jesus cannot use us. Imagine Him sitting on His throne observing us and thinking, "I am in need of a Bible Training teacher for the stewardship class. Who can I trust to fill that position? Oh yes, John has proven himself faithful as a cell group leader, and he knows I have called him to teach. He has also been a faithful giver and manager of his money, and knows what it is like to get out of debt. I'll suggest his name to the department head right now!"

Can we trust Jesus to promote us and help us to grow in His own time? Suppose John decided to toot his own horn and pester the department head, trying to promote himself? He would probably get ahead of the Lord and out of His timing. He might find himself in a teaching position that did not suit him.

The key to true spiritual growth is *preparation*. Jesus uses people who are prepared to serve Him and to receive the harvest that results from service. He is fair, just, and will not waste a willing servant who is prepared.

Scripture Meditations

Colossians 1:15-19

Philippians 4:19

Colossians 2:2-3

Ephesians 1:22-23

Thought Provokers

Serving Jesus Christ involves creating new ideas and plans. List three new ways you can do this in your ministry.

1.

2.

3.

If you want God to give the increase in your ministry, what do you need to do to prepare for that increase?

Chapter 14

Proper Attitude In Leadership

The dictionary defines "attitude" as "a way of acting or behaving that shows what one is thinking or feeling." As I mentioned previously, the *Harvard Business Review* says that the reason a person gets a job and keeps it is 85% *attitude* and only 15% *aptitude*. It is strange then that most companies spend almost their entire training budget on technical and skill development? The development of a proper attitude is much more important!

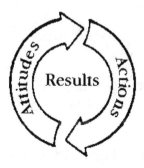

The Bible has much to say about the development of right attitudes. Let's look at two passages of Scripture:

Be constantly renewed in the spirit of your mind-having a fresh mental and spiritual ATTITUDE.

—Ephesians 4:23 (Amplified)

Do not be conformed to this world — this age, fashioned after and adapted to its external, superficial customs. But be transformed (changed) by the (entire) renewal of your mind — by its new ideals and its new ATTITUDE — so that you may prove for yourself what is the good and acceptable and perfect will of God. . .

— *Romans 12:2 (Amplified)*

A sparkling, faith-filled attitude is fundamental to success in leadership. Our actions stem from our attitudes and our leadership success will be the result of a whole string of right actions.

An improper attitude will exhibit negative signs, which we should be careful to weed out of our own lives. Here are some of them:

1. Self-pity. "Some people have all of the lucky breaks. . . but not me." "I'm too old." "I'm too young." "There aren't any jobs out there." "I've got the wrong education."

2. Fatalism. "That's the way the ball bounces." "That's the way the cookie crumbles."

3. Magnifying the negative. Dwelling on the daily bad news and blowing it way out of proportion.

4. Downplaying the positive. "How did he get promoted to manager? He really isn't that smart!" "That pastor draws crowds because he preaches that 'prosperity' gospel."

5. Taking everything personally. "I overhead a group of people mention my name and laugh."

6. Looking at partially negative situations as totally negative. "I understand a few of our people left town and joined a cult. Must be I'm not ministering to people correctly."

7. Jumping to conclusions. "I hear they are laying off people. I guess I better get prepared for it now."

I once knew a business manager, whom I will call Mr. Fognozzle. Although he was technically brilliant, he had a negative attitude. He tried to make himself look important by downplaying the achievements of those who worked with him. As a result, he was not respected by his coworkers, and the negative attitude spread throughout the department. Usually, people would avoid Mr. Fognozzle to keep from having to deal with him. Productivity in his department suffered.

The success or failure of a business, ministry department, or church will be determined greatly by the attitude of the leadership. Studies reveal the following statistics for churches, businesses, ministries, and salesmen: 5% are super successful, 15% are medium successful, and 80% are somewhere between mediocre and failing.

A direct correlation was found among the successful leaders of these various enterprises. The difference between the super successful and the rest was not in education or skill. Often you will find the more successful men and women are, the less educated many of them are. The whole difference is found in only one major area: *ATTITUDES!* Leaders with super, faith-filled *attitudes* attract the right results! Attitudes! They affect everything in our lives!

Scripture Meditations

> 1 Peter 4:1
>
> Numbers 13 and 14
>
> Romans 12:1-2
>
> Isaiah 43:18-19
>
> Joshua 14:10-11

Thought Provokers

In this section we listed the signs of improper attitude. Now turn those completely around and list the signs of a proper attitude for leadership:

1. He makes no excuses.

2. He accepts full responsibility for his results.

3. Magnifies the positive.

Chapter 15

The Process Of Mind Renewal

And do not be conformed to this world, but be transformed by the renewing of your mind, that you may prove what is that good and acceptable and perfect will of God.

— Romans 12:2

Since the fall of man (Genesis 3:1-24), the natural tendency for all of creation is to drift downhill into decay and disorder. This includes our thought processes. It is easy to write a computer program with bugs in it. Similarly, it is natural for our minds to receive "wrong programming" and our thoughts to become polluted.

We have been programmed for years by the world; with myths, folklore, lies, and false concepts. Now, we must daily "key in" the proper program based upon God's Word. The Bible teaches that man is a trichotomy; a little trinity, consisting of spirit,

soul, and body. The soul is the area of the mind. In fact, the two words soul and mind are usually synonymous. The spirit is instantly reborn when a person accepts Jesus Christ — it is an instantaneous event. Renewing the mind, however, is a progressive operation, and must go on continuously. In the Greek language, the word "renew" carries a picture of renovation. When you renovate an old dilapidated house, you remove all of the old useless parts and step-by-step replace them with new parts: plumbing, fixtures, wallpaper, paint. In time, the house is no longer recognizable as the same structure. It has been renovated — renewed!

There are many hindrances to the mind renewal process. Be careful to avoid these:

1. **Hypnotism**

2. **Illicit drugs** (cocaine, hash, marijuana, alcohol, etc.)

3. **Lack of rest**

4. **Occultism** (Spiritism, Ouija boards, astrology — see Deuteronomy 18:9-15)

5. **Negative self-talk** ("I am no good," "I will never be a good leader.")

6. **Some secular songs**

These hindrances clutter the mind with confusion, trapping people into bondage and defeat. For example, listen to the words of a secular song: "I've

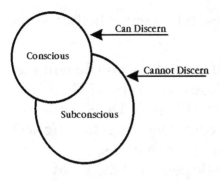

got heartaches by the number, troubles by the score . . ." I sure do not want that negative influence running around in my mind over and over. I know people who regularly listen to secular radio stations and consistently become depressed and full of problems. They do not realize that it's the ungodly lyrics that are "programming" them at a subconscious level. A song that was popular several years ago began with this line: "It's a hard world to get a break in. All the good things have been taken." If you allow your mind to take this in at a subconscious level, you will find it more difficult to become a successful leader. Do you want to renew your mind? Here's how:

1. Read the Bible *daily* (Especially the New Testament). Meditate on a verse or two for at least three weeks (21 days) at a time. Take only a bite-size portion of scripture, but read it daily, think about it, memorize it, say it, get it into you.

2. Make a habit of listening to Bible tapes, whenever possible. Also, get some good, faith-filled,

teaching tapes and listen to them, whether or not you feel like it.

3. Begin to act as if everything you do will succeed. Do you share Jesus with others? Do it with total faith that success will result. Do you pray for the sick? Do it with confidence that healing will follow. Make a habit of being a positive, peppy, faith-filled, enthusiastic person of the Word.

4. Take out the junk. Rid yourself of bad habits, negative input, and false ideas that clutter your mind and hinder your walk with Jesus. If you follow these steps, you will find your mind being renovated. As a result, more and more success in your leadership and ministry will follow.

Scripture Meditations

John 6:63

Ephesians 4:22-24

Romans 12:1-2

Philippians 4:13

Thessalonians 5:23

Thought Provokers

What are some of the worldly thought patterns that Christians can develop if they are not staying in God's Word?

Ask your pastor for a list of excellent books you should read or tapes you should listen to in order to aid in your mind renewal process. List them:

"Show me a man who cannot bother to do little things and I'll show you a man who cannot be trusted to do big things."

— *Lawrence D. Bell*

Chapter 16

Beware Of The Deadly Sin Of Excuse-itis

"Excuse-itis" is a disease of the unrenewed mind. Its root cause is unbelief. Let me give you some examples of excuse-itis. In Numbers 13 and 14, twelve spies were sent to survey the Land of Promise. When they brought back their reports to Moses, ten of the spies "brought up an evil report of the land." They had a failure attitude! They could not see beyond the giants that inhabited the land. These spies became living failures. The two with faith attitudes said, "We can go into the Promised Land because God told us we could, and He will fight for us!" These two spies became living legends of success and victory. Their names? Joshua and Caleb.

I was told by a recognized church leader that there could never be a powerful church in Lansing, Michigan because the city had a "Samson spirit." (I never asked what he meant by that.) Now, if I believed that bit about the "Samson spirit," I would never have even prayed for a successful, growing church in the city of Lansing. Instead, I reasoned, "If this man wants to focus on the Samson spirit (whatever that is), let him go ahead. I'll focus on the Holy Spirit and, with God's grace and help, build a powerful, praying, growing ministry and church in the city of Lansing, Michigan." We did it! Glory to God! Watch out for excuse-itis.

Another minister told me there would never be another growing church in Lansing because this other church "has everything all tied up." I shook my head in disbelief. The church he was referring to had 700 members. At the time, our church had only 300 or so. Today, that minister and his church are gone. Failed! Folded! Why? Because he was a bad individual? No. He was a good man, but he had come down with the disease of excuse-itis. He made excuses for failure instead of aiming for success. Our church (at the time of this writing) has over 4,000 members. When you are preaching the gospel, the number of "prospects" is unlimited.

Have you heard these excuses?

"There are no jobs out there." (See Mark 9:23.)

"I'm too old now." (See Joshua 14:10-11.)

"I'm too young." (Jeremiah was only 17.)

"But I've failed in the past." (See Isaiah 43:18-19.)

"But I have the wrong education." (See Acts 4:13.)

The Word of God will strip away all excuses for not moving ahead in power and anointing! Do not let excuse-itis ruin your ministry.

Scripture Meditations

Mark 9:23

Philippians 3:13

Joshua 14:10-11

Acts 4:13

Jeremiah 1:5-9

Luke 14:16-24

Isaiah 43:18-19

Thought Provokers

Have you ever made an excuse for some failure in your life or ministry?

List some excuses you are going to have to overcome:

What plan do you have for curing "excuse-itis" in your life?

Chapter 17

What Kind Of Leader Is God Looking For?

Many people called by God into leadership are afraid because they are imperfect. I struggled with this myself. I wanted to wait until I had reached the ultimate in personal, practical holiness before I did anything for God. As I read and studied God's Word, something occurred to me. The people God called "perfect" were certainly not what I would call perfect.

Abraham, God's friend, told a half-truth in order to save his own neck. David, a man after God's heart, lusted after a married woman, then committed adultery and murder. Job, a "perfect" man, allowed his life to be riddled with fear.

Even the disciples who walked with our Lord, displayed evidence that they still needed some sanctification! Temper tantrums, prejudice, false revelations, denying Christ, and even arguing among themselves marked just a few of the imperfections we find in the Lord's first apostles. As I read God's Word, I discovered an important principle: *God's not looking for perfect people, but people with perfect hearts toward Him.* God's men of the Bible, with the exception of our Lord Jesus, were not perfect in the sense that they had attained a pinnacle of personal holiness. However, they did all have one thing in common: they had perfect hearts toward God. This is not to say that they did not have to let the Holy Ghost give them a heart checkup from time to time, but overall, they loved God!

Read these scriptures and see if you come to the same conclusion.

Scripture Meditations

> 2 Kings 20:3
>
> 2 Chronicles 16:9
>
> 1 Chronicles 28:9
>
> Psalm 101:4
>
> 1 Chronicles 29:9
>
> Matthew 5:48
>
> 1 Chronicles 29:19
>
> Galatians 3:3

Thought Provokers

Have you held back from some calling of God on your life because of a real or perceived imperfection?

Are your willing to yield that imperfection to the Holy Spirit so He can help you develop in holiness?

Are you willing to answer God's call now?

What steps are you going to take from here?

"A man who wants to lead the orchestra must turn his back on the crowd."

— *James Crook*

Chapter 18

Surrender To Doing Things God's Way

Human pride always wants to prove itself. Human pride must bow its knee to the plan of God. God's ways are not our ways.

Moses tried to do things his way and failed until he was willing to hear from God and do things His way. Then he became a super-success.

A young Christian man fresh out of college and newly married was faced with the draft and decided to join the Navy. He was placed in a classification that was in conflict with the training he had in college. Frustrated, he started complaining, and soon he was in a bit of trouble. Little did he realize that God allowed him to be placed in that job so that he could remain with his wife during that time. He got shore duty in San Diego, then two years later he was assigned to a ship coming into the yards for repairs. He never did go to sea! Not until he was well into the shore duty did he realize what God was doing for him to keep him close to his wife. He could have saved himself some grief if he had trusted the Lord completely during that time.

Bloom where you are planted. If things are not the way you think they should be in your situation, make the best of the resources you have and keep trusting Jesus. God made you and you belong to Him. Will He, being a perfect God, steer you in the wrong direction —of course not. Learn to hear His voice and do everything His way.

Scripture Meditations

Proverbs 3:5-6

Isaiah 55:6-9

Thought Provokers

What have you been trying to do in your own way, only to meet repeated failure?

How can you bloom where you are planted right now?

Chapter 19

Make Time And Get In The Habit Of Studying

A perfect heart toward God is exhibited in a surrendered attitude and a studying mind. What should a leader and minister study? God's Word, the Bible! He should also study other books written by master teachers in the body of Christ. Paul studied the Bible and other books too (2 Timothy 4:13).

How do we become perfect?

All scripture is given by inspiration of God, and is profitable for doctrine, for reproof, for correction, for instruction in righteousness: That the man of God may be perfect, thoroughly furnished unto all good works.

— 2 Timothy 3:16-17

When we grow in God's Word, the Bible, we grow in perfection, completely equipped for the ministry.

Do you feel that everyone else is smarter than you? It's not true, so do not be overwhelmed. We learn little by little, here a little and there a little. We can speed the process up by the amount of time we invest in reading and studying.

> *Who shall teach knowledge? and whom shall he make to understand doctrine? Them that are weaned from the milk, and drawn from the breasts. For precept must be upon precept, line upon line; here a little, and there a little.*
>
> *—Isaiah 28:9-10*

You may ask, "How can I study?" Here are some personal tips:

1. Have a special place to study daily. It may be a spare room, a corner of the basement, a garage, attic, or just about anyplace you can be alone regularly with God.

2. Sanctify your area. Pray over it. Use it only for prayer and study.

3. Make sure you have enough light. A dim light will make you feel drowsy and tired.

4. Use pens, pencils, and highlighters as you read. Mark important passages. Develop your own color code system.

5. Study twelve to fifteen major topics per year. For example:

ANGELS, INTERCESSION, BITTERNESS, PROPHECY, CHARACTER, PRAISE, DEPRESSION,

SUCCESS, FAITH, TEACHING, GUIDANCE, and WISDOM.

If you try to study more than twelve to fifteen topics in one year, you will likely become discouraged and have little material under each subject. When I started a regular Bible study method, I made the mistake of developing a file with 178 topics. Needless to say, it failed miserably. The next year, however, I kept a file on only fifteen subjects. The result was phenomenal. I had enough material to write four full-size books, teach for a year, plus, have reference materials for unlimited years to come.

6. Become a reader. Empty hearts are not fed by empty heads. A reader will likely become a leader. I read 112 books my first year in the ministry. I now read about 50 books a year. Study leads to stability! Leaders must be stable-minded. If we want to prevent ourselves from double-mindedness, we need to "study to show ourselves approved unto God, a workman that needeth not be ashamed, rightly dividing the word of truth," (2 Timothy 2:15).

Scripture Meditations

> 2 Timothy 4:13
>
> 2 Timothy 3:16-17
>
> 2 Timothy 2:15-16
>
> Isaiah 28:9-10

Thought Provokers

Starting now, what are you going to do to develop a better life of study?

Write out your plan for developing better study habits:

Chapter 20

How To Develop Stability

When Christians study, one of the results is that they settle down and their lives become stable. Many Christians are moody, up and down, making them very volatile. Operating constantly by feelings, they are more like a reed blowing in the wind than a tree planted by the water (Psalms 1). Thus, God can use them only in a limited capacity. We do not feel like doing what we should 80% of the time, but what do feelings have to do with it? We do what we should because it's right, not because we feel like it.

"Roller coaster" Christians have good intentions, but their impulsiveness, lack of consistency

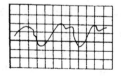

"Roller-coaster" Christians

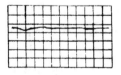

Stable Christians

and unpredictability prevents God from promoting them.

We all need to understand: *Reliability* and *dependability* are more important than ability. By studying God's Word on a consistent basis, we learn how to discern that which is genuinely spiritual and that which is purely emotional and feelings oriented.

> For the word of God is quick, and powerful, and sharper than any two edged sword, piercing even to the dividing asunder of the joints and marrow, and is a discerner of the thoughts and intents of the heart.
>
> — Hebrews 4:12

Emotional preachers make emotional converts. When the emotional tidal wave recedes, the new "converts" recede with it. That's why stable preachers get people to commit their lives to Jesus Christ because it's the right thing to do, not just because of some sad, tear-jerking story.

God wants Christians to come to the place where they do things because they are the right things to do, not because they have special "feelings" or "inspiration."

An expert pianist would laugh at the novice who says, "I will practice when the inspiration comes." An expert writer would laugh when a beginner says, "I will write when the mood strikes me." God's not looking for perfect people. He is looking to promote stable people — those who are reliable and dependable.

Scripture Meditations

Hebrews 4:12

2 Corinthians 4:2

Thought Provokers

In what ways can you develop a deeper stability in your life?

List the times this week you have made decisions based upon "feelings" rather than what was right.

"Leadership is the capacity to translate vision into reality."

— *Warren G. Bennis*

Chapter 21

The Power Of A Vision

It is not enough to be stable. You need vision and direction. A hunter went out in the woods one day with his shotgun and started to shoot aimlessly in all directions. His companion ran for cover. When the din stopped and the dust settled, he ran up, tackled his friend, took his gun away from him and demanded to know what he was doing. "I'm hunting. If I shoot all over the place, I'm bound to hit something!"

Some Christians are like that! Even though they have accepted Jesus as their Savior, they have not yet received a vision for their lives. As a consequence, they are shooting off in all directions, hoping to hit something. Like the mad hunter, they cannot take the time to wait for something to

Stay on Target

shoot. So, they try this and try that, hoping to find success in something or other. Is it any wonder that so many fail?

Three Things That Cause Failure

Take a look at the following three causes of failure. Why do you think they cause defeat?

1. Lack of vision

2. Lack of knowledge

3. Lack of obedience

Turning that around, what do you suppose are three great keys to success?

1. Vision

2. Knowledge

3. Obedience

If you want to succeed at hunting, you first need a target. Without a goal, or a vision of the game you want to hunt, it is useless to shoot the gun, and very dangerous.

If you lack knowledge in the handling of the gun, or do not obey simple rules of safety, you are not likely to hit your target even though you have something at which to aim.

> *Where there is no vision, the people perish: but he that keepeth the law, happy is he.*
>
> *— Proverbs 29:18*

Vision, knowledge, and obedience work hand in hand to help you to succeed as a leader. Without any one of the three, you are bound to fail. If you remove one of the legs of a three legged stool and try to sit on it, you will collapse. Similarly, you could have the vision for a ministry, and have the knowledge how to do it, but if you cannot obey those in authority over you or the leading of the Holy Spirit, your ministry will fail.

In the same manner, if you have a vision, and want to obey God, but do not prepare yourself with the proper knowledge and study, you will fail in your endeavor. Now let's talk about vision. The person of faith will see things that others cannot see (2 Corinthians 4:18). A faith vision is a general target that we aim for, one that comes from God. I call it a "faith movie".

Scripture References

John 4:35

2 Corinthians 4:18

Hebrews 11:1, 27

Proverbs 29:18

Thought Provokers

What is vision, and where does it come from?

What does knowledge have to do with vision?

What part does obedience play with vision and knowledge?

What can you do to focus on the vision God has given you, and can you give examples of what aimlessness is?

Chapter 22

The Importance Of A Vision

People perish without a vision. In Samuel's day there was no shared vision (1 Samuel 3:1). Not knowing what God wanted them to do, everyone did what was right in their own eyes. "Oh, I think this is what the Lord wants." "Maybe this is the right thing to do." "No, I think God wants it this way." The end result was destruction and bondage for the children of Israel.

Not seeing the plan God has for us makes us vulnerable to Satan's plan. In fact, if you have no vision for your life, guess what? Without a doubt, you are accomplishing Satan's vision.

There is a way which seemeth right unto a man, but the end thereof are the ways of death.

—Proverbs 14:12

This verse is so important, it is repeated in Proverbs 16:25. That which "seems right" in our own eyes can be our destruction.

We are often tempted to take shortcuts around the solution God wants to implement. Such shortcuts are dangerous. It is never a good idea to get ahead of God, or try to substitute our ideas for His.

A young man took a trip out west to go to college in Wyoming. Near Chicago, he ran into a blinding thunderstorm and his vision was impaired. After the storm cleared, he realized he was 150 miles out of his way until he started seeing signs for St. Louis, not Des Moines. The road did not look any different, it *seemed* right, but he was lost just the same.

Likewise, we can stray off the path God has given us during the storms of life, and not even realize it. But, praise God, vision can get us back on the road, going in the right direction. Being lost is not fun. Having no vision is a tragedy. Most people find themselves in that situation at one time or another. When there is no vision, everyone loses.

A young recruit in the Navy found himself appointed leader of a platoon, and was told to march everyone over to the classroom. After twenty minutes of marching around the compound, with ten other sailors marching faithfully behind him, he finally had to admit he did not know where the classroom was. If you do not know where you are going, do not try to be a leader. If the blind lead the blind, they will both fall into a ditch.

Scripture Meditations

> 1 Samuel 3:1
>
> Proverbs 14:12
>
> 1 Kings 11:33-35
>
> Psalm 119:105
>
> Micah 3:5-7

Thought Provokers

Can you think of a time you thought you were doing what was right, but got in trouble anyway?

How can you know whether or not the path you are taking is the correct one?

If you stray from the path God has called you to, how can you get back on track?

Are you "in the groove" or in a rut?

"If you want a track team to win the high jump, you find one person who can jump seven feet, not seven people who can jump one foot."

— *Louis Terman*

Chapter 23

Church Programs Must Have A Specific Mission

One of the reasons some churches do not grow and expand is because of lack of direction and vision. If an automobile manufacturing company decided that each of its workers could do whatever they wanted to do, the entire car assembly process would break down. One worker would want to make stove parts, another computer parts, another truck parts, and so on. We can only imagine what kind of contraption would come out the end of the assembly line.

In the same sense, churches manufacture a product: new Christians. If the church is not producing new Christians, and the new Christians are not producing fruit, we have failed in our mission.

We as a church have a threefold mission:

W — Worship (Ministry to God)

E — Evangelism (Ministry to the world)

B — Building of the Saints (Ministry to the believers)

We refer to this as the "WEB" principle: W-E-B. If a program in the church does not have one of these three purposes as its primary goal, it should be revamped or dissolved.

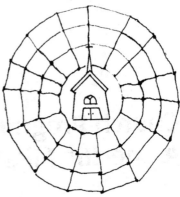

These are examples: "bizarres", socials, tea parties, garden clubs, etc. Any of these, under the right direction, could produce fruit if the WEB was the goal, but more often than not, they become ends to themselves. Why put money and man hours into something which does not produce fruit?

If any aspect of your "ministry" does not fall into one or more of the categories of Worship, Evangelism, or Building of the Saints, it's time to reevaluate it. An apple tree periodically needs to have dead branches pruned in order for it to produce good fruit. If a church program or ministry is not producing good fruit, it's no doubt draining other ministries. Cut it off!

One of the biggest problems with pruning is when the people involved in these church programs have made them their pet projects, and are offended if you cut "their" program. But, that is part of the seed principle we learned about earlier. Except a kernel of wheat die, it cannot produce fruit. When a program is discontinued, let the people involved know that it may someday grow back to full flower and produce good fruit. God frequently does this when He finds someone with the proper vision and commitment for it. If you are ever in the delicate situation where you have to cut a church program or ministry that is not producing fruit, keep this in mind. Encourage the people involved to give the ministry time to sprout and grow again. It's the resurrection principle.

The most common problem in the church is not having any direction at all. Consequently, much of our valuable time is wasted chasing trivialities that have no bearing on reaching people for Jesus Christ. Having a specific mission for your church helps you decide which of your priorities are most important so you do not go off on a tangent. This principle holds true for your personal life as well. Once you decide what is truly important and lasting in your life, it is easy to make decisions and choices.

For example, what Christian does not have the problem of sorting out appeals for support from many worthy ministries? How do we deal with this? By finding out what our specific mission is, and supporting the ministries that fit in with that mission. That cuts out the clutter and makes our decision making easier.

Scripture Meditations

John 12:24

1 Corinthians 3:9-15

Matthew 13:3-23

Matthew 5:29-30

Thought Provokers

Can you think of any program in your church that is not producing fruit? Why?

List ministries in the church that fall in the following categories: Worship, Evangelism, Building of the Saints.

Is there anything in your ministry that is not producing fruit?

What can you do about it?

Chapter 24

True Vision Is Born In Prayer

What is prayer? Prayer is sometimes defined as the transfer of God's ideas without the stain of human logic. When God gives you a vision, you do not need to understand how it will be fulfilled —not yet. Human logic will tend to rob you of your vision. Your mind will tell you, "It's not logical." "Where will you get the money?" "You're not qualified." "How are you going to do that?" Trying to figure it all out can destroy your vision. Instead, get God's vision clear in your mind, and He shows you how it will be accomplished in microsegments.

Be careful with whom you share your vision. Some people think that their role in life is to "bring you back down to reality." Don't even think about whispering a hint of it to them! Find someone who is not quick to pass judgment, who has a healthy imagination, and share your thoughts with them.

There are two different basic types of vision:

1. Mental (Sight)

2. Supernatural Revelation

We think in pictures. Close your eyes and imagine a cute little poodle. What do you see? You do not see the letters, "C-U-T-E L-I-T-T-L-E P-O-O-D-L-E", you see a picture. This is mental-sight. The word imagination really means *image*-ination or picturing an image in your mind. As you pray, activate your imagination. Let the Lord direct the pictures of what He wants you to do. Go over it in your mind. Use this formula: PRAYER - VISION - PRAYER - VISION. What you see by faith is more real than what you see by sight.

Another kind of vision God will give us is Supernatural revelation.

> *And it shall come to pass in the last days, saith God, I pour out my spirit upon all flesh: and your sons and your daughters shall prophesy, and your young men shall see visions, and your old men shall dream dreams: And on my servants and on my handmaidens I will pour out in those days of my Spirit; and they shall prophesy.*

> *—Acts 2:17-18*

Supernatural revelation is for today. Why is it that some people attribute everything supernatural to the devil? Something concerns me deeply about this. There are a few preachers who feel that visions, dreams, or anything supernatural is of the devil or the occult. Did God all of a sudden choose to strip himself of all power and allow the devil free reign in the realm of the supernatural? No, God's gifts, power, and might are still freely available to all who ask for them. Yes, visions, prophecy, and all of the gifts can be imitated by the devil. But do not let that blind you. Keep seeking God for the genuine. Do not be fooled by the counterfeit. People do not stop spending money just because they might find a counterfeit $20 bill. Do not reject spiritual gifts because Satan mocks them with his own phony imitations.

When you pray and seek vision and revelation from God, it helps to do a little "creative loafing." God cannot give us vision while we are always busy, busy, busy, running here, running there, trying to "do something" for the Lord. What the Lord wants you to "do" is to be still and listen. That was the purpose of the Sabbath. God gave us a time just to lie around, loaf, and draw near to Him. It is during that time that God will speak to us and give us direction. Do not give God a "busy" signal.

Scripture Meditations

Acts 2:17-18

John 4:35

1 Corinthians 14:39

2 Corinthians 4:18

Thought Provokers

List three statements you hear people make which destroys visions.

What is the difference between a mental picture and supernatural revelation?

Give an example of a genuine supernatural revelation and one that is counterfeit.

What is "creative loafing?"

Chapter 25

The Principle Of The Big Picture

A bread truck hit a bump as it traveled down the highway, and spilled some of its contents on the side of the road. Then, a flock of birds saw the pile of crumbs and began to scramble after it. The birds fought over the scraps, pecking each other, feathers flying. However, one bird chose not to participate. Instead, he flew up high over the highway to get a bird's eye view of the situation. What do you suppose he saw? Like a miracle, there it was: a whole loaf of bread on the side of the road, overlooked by the other birds who were in the middle of the fight. He swooped down and got the whole loaf all to himself! Now there was one bird who ended up fat and happy!

VISION
(BIG PICTURE)

How did he do it? Instead of fighting over mere crumbs, he climbed up and got an aerial view of the whole situation. He got the *big picture*. That is what vision will do for you. It will give you a broad picture of God's overall plan so that you do not waste your time on peripheral issues.

Without a vision, people end up taking Scriptures out of context and picking apart issues that do not amount to much. One person came to me and told me that puppets were displeasing to God. He had some Scripture that he took out of context to prove his idea. Another took Jeremiah 10:2-4 to mean that Christmas trees are pagan. Such ideas are the result of not having the complete picture. Many people waste their time on little gripes and crazy ideas which amount to very little for the cause of Christ.

Lack of vision also will cause you to give up before your time. Florence Chadwick had the dream of swimming from Santa Catalina Island to Long Beach. This 26 mile swim was hazardous, with cold treacherous currents. Only 1/2 mile from her goal, she called for the boat and quit. If she had seen that she was so close, she was sure she could have made it.

How often do we give up because we do not have the total picture, but instead we see the wind, current and waves? Sometimes people are misled by an incomplete or outdated vision. Two men stopped their pickup truck at a gas station on US-

30 in Nebraska to ask for directions. The attendant asked them where they were going. "We're headed for San Francisco!" They replied. "Why don't you get on Interstate 80, just a few miles down this road?" "Interstate 80? Where is that?" they replied. Come to find out, the map they were using was dated 1959. They were lost because they were trying to follow an outdated map, taking routes that had changed long ago. In the same way, old traditional ways of doing things in the church, although once valid, can lead people astray or are ineffective because the times are different. Make sure your inner map, which is your *vision*, is up to date.

Vision is your inner instrument that gives you guidance while flying through cloudy skies. A pilot saw airport lights below him through the clouds. Thinking it was the airport where he was to land, he did not believe his instruments that told him otherwise. As he descended below the clouds, he saw that it was not his airport after all, it was Camp Pendleton. He quickly climbed back up, but it was too late. The marines got his number and reported him to the FAA. He should have believed his instruments. Believe your inner instruments of vision. Remember, your sight does not give you the total picture. Walk by faith, not by sight.

Scripture Meditations

> 2 Corinthians 5:7
>
> Genesis 15:1-6
>
> 2 Corinthians 12:1-4
>
> Acts 10:9-48
>
> Acts 18:9-10
>
> Daniel 7, 8

Thought Provokers

What are some of the things you can do to get an aerial view of your situation?

What kinds of issues that are common in the church display lack of vision, and tend to spoil things rather than accomplish God's purpose? Give some examples.

Give an example of a technique that was used in the past to win souls for Christ, but is ineffective now because the times are different.

Have you ever given up too soon on your vision? Why?

Chapter 26

If You Can See The Invisible, You Can Accomplish The Impossible

It is impossible to accomplish God's will without a vision. That is why miracles seem impossible to people: they lack vision. With a vision, God's people can accomplish the impossible.

If you take a jigsaw puzzle and dump all 1000 pieces out onto the table, it does not just fall together. That's impossible! But, if you put it together, piece by piece, using the picture on the box as a pattern, it will soon become a beautiful picture. If God tells you His plan, it does not matter how many people say it is impossible, *you can do it!*

Let's take a look at some people who had a vision given to them by God, and accomplished the impossible. Hebrews chapter 11 gives us plenty of examples.

Verse 4: Abel offered a more excellent sacrifice than Cain because he had the vision of what God's ultimate plan was.

Verse 5: Enoch, by his faith, was translated that he should not see death. His testimony was that he pleased God.

Verse 7: By faith, Noah built his ark and escaped the judgment of the world. Through him, his house was saved and he became the heir of the righteousness that is by faith.

Verse 8-10: Abraham obeyed God and was called to go out into a strange land where he was to receive an inheritance from God.

Verse 11: Sarah conceived and delivered a son, Isaac, even though she was past age.

Verse 17-19: Abraham offered Isaac up to God in sacrifice, knowing that God was able to raise him up again if necessary, to fulfill his promise.

Verse 20: Isaac blessed Jacob and Esau.

Verse 22: Joseph foretold Israel's departure from Egypt before he died.

Verse 23: Moses was hidden by his parents because they saw the vision God had for him.

Verse 24-28: When Moses matured, he refused to be called the son of Pharaoh's daughter, choosing to suffer affliction with his people rather than to enjoy the pleasures of sin for a season.

As you look at each of these, ask yourself this question: How did they apply *vision, knowledge* and *obedience* in their lives?

Study this Bible chapter and find out how God gave vision to these people, who "obtained a good report through faith." God gave each of them a vision and equipped them for the ministry because they were obedient.

The impossible can be accomplished! With men it is impossible, but with God, all things are possible, because it is He who supplies the need. The reason most people do not see miracles is because of their limited view of the power of God: They are blind to the miracles all around them.

Miracles are so commonplace, they are taken for granted. They are not recognized as God's intervention in our lives. Take for instance the process that takes place when a cut finger heals. You would not expect your car to automatically heal if you gash the paint job with a knife. God has built in a wonderful repair mechanism in your body so that if you have a cut, it will heal. How much more can we expect God to intervene in our lives! We are sons and daughters created by the most high God! Why would He withhold His good purpose from those who love Him?

Scripture Meditations

Hebrews 11

Genesis 24

Genesis 37:5-11

1 Samuel 16:1-13

Thought Provokers

Why do people doubt the existence of miracles?

Does God have a miracle for you? What is it?

What did all of the people mentioned in Hebrews 11 have in common?

Chapter 27

Learn How To Set Faith Goals

Once you have a vision — then what? How can you make your vision come to pass? By setting and reaching FAITH GOALS. A vision is like a masterpiece painting, and faith goals are like the brush strokes. They are small steps that go in to making the big picture. That is how a vision is accomplished.

Failure to plan and set goals is the greatest source of long term failures in any organization. It is a vital stage to any project. If you do not plan, you quickly discover that circumstances, problems, situations, and other people will determine your priorities. Mapping out a schedule prevents "crisis management" and "fire fight-

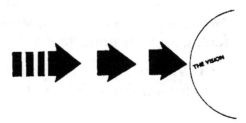

ing." With a plan, you know where you are going, what you are going to do, and when it should take place.

Statistics tell us that 98% of all project failures are the result of improper planning. You would not consider building a house without a blueprint. Why start a project without a plan? If God has given you a dream, do not launch into it haphazardly. A home builder does not plan the house he is building as he works on it. "Oh, I think now I'll put in a bathroom." "A bedroom might look nice here." "Oops, now the plumbing doesn't fit, I'll have to reroute it over here." "OH NO! I forgot the basement." Such a house, which is nothing but a series of additions and changes, usually ends up looking peculiar . . . to say the least.

Use your time to plan productively. Plan your day, plan your week, plan your month, plan your year. Plan your business, plan your ministry, and plan to see your dreams come true. Count on God to direct you.

How To Plan

Planning with the direction of the Lord involves two steps: *defining your vision* and *setting faith goals*. A vision and a goal are distinctively different, and it is important to know the difference.

1. Vision: An overall picture that can be pursued for indefinite times in the future.

2. Goal: A target to aim at within our planning period that will move us closer to realizing our God-given vision.

A vision is general, a goal is specific. You must first know what you want before you can plan for it. God has given a plan and a purpose for each of his children. A good way to define your vision specifically is to write it out on a sheet of paper. After you have done that, read it out loud, study it, ask for God's guidance and revise it over and over. Do not try to understand it or figure it all out in this first stage. Simply trust God in faith to direct you. The important thing is to *know what your vision is.*

My life's vision is to lead people into a deeper, more fruitful fellowship with the Lord Jesus Christ, and to inspire them to use their faith in reaching their greatest potential for Him. There you have it. That's my basic dream; my vision.

Consider writing your vision down on paper. When you can define your vision and get it on paper, God will begin to give you faith goals and ideas that will help you accomplish your vision.

The reason some people are not getting anywhere is because they do not know where they are going. They interview for a job and say "Oh, I will do anything." To an interviewer, that is a red flag. If they do not specifically know what they want, how can they have a skill?

Once you have put your vision down on paper, the next step is to set faith goals. If you were to conduct a personal survey on the street, asking people their specific goals, only four to five percent would be able to tell you in direct concise terms what their goals in life are. The other 95% would have no goals at all or only general dreams such as "to be happy" or "to be healthy." This is like going to the airport and asking for a ticket at the airline counter. "I'd like an airline ticket, please." "What is your destination, sir?" asks the airline clerk. "Oh, I don't know. Anywhere I guess. Just give me a ticket." Does that sound a little foolish? How many individuals try to gain success in life without even knowing where they want to go, and without setting clear cut goals for getting anywhere? It's a little like getting on a merry-go-round. You push it around and around in a circle, get it going real fast, expend a lot of energy, but never really get anyplace.

Having no concrete goals is like having a captain of an ocean liner decide to set out to sea with no spe-  cific port in mind. "Well, I just thought we would drift along today, and see where the tide takes us.

Hopefully, we will end up in the right port." The chances are of that happening are about sixteen trillion to one. That's what happens when you do not have any specific goals. You will drift through life, hoping to arrive somewhere. More often than not, you will end up on the rocks.

It is also important to make your faith goals *specific*. During the night, a cabin cruiser approached the channel at Pentwater, Michigan. Realizing he had missed it, he turned around for another approach, hit the pier and sank. What was his problem? He did not center his attention on where he was, and found himself off course and on the rocks.

Faith goals are micro segments of the total picture. They are definite, distinctive and clear. Do not make up nebulous goals that are too general. That is not faith. Instead, get specific: What plans have you made for your vision in life?

Scripture **Meditations**

Proverbs 8:29

1 Corinthians 9:23

Mark 9:23

Mark 11:24

Hebrews 11:1

Thought **Provokers**

What is a plan? What is the difference between a vision and a goal?

If your vision is to build a Bible college in Brazil, what would be the specific goals you would have to reach in order for you to accomplish it?

Write out what your God-given vision is.

Chapter 28

What Is A Goal?

A goal is a checkpoint on your journey through life. It is a specific target for you to reach within a period of time along the way of making your God-given vision come true. If you do not learn to set clear cut goals, you probably will never rise above mediocrity. Rather than have your life just float with the circumstances, set your mark toward the high calling of Christ Jesus.

A man had a vision to explore the rivers and seacoast of America by canoe. He laid out his plan for a 25,000 mile route which went down the St. Lawrence Seaway, down the Atlantic coast, up the Mississippi River, up the Mackenzie River in the Arctic to Alaska, down the Pacific coast to Baja, California, up the Colorado River, down the Missouri and back to the Great Lakes. His motto was "The impossible only takes a little longer!"

Having accomplished that incredible journey, his new vision was to paddle his canoe from the Arctic Ocean all the way to the tip of South America.

How did he accomplish his objective? He had a schedule to meet with checkpoints along the way. He had to plan for the weather and the seasons, portages around waterfalls, and physical conditioning. In order for him to realize his goal, it took planning, preparation and forethought to overcome obstacles.

What if he just set out in his canoe and decided to go wherever he felt like it? He probably would not get very far before he ran into disaster. Instead, he was able to accomplish what others deemed impossible.

As the first person to canoe *up* the Colorado river, he made this journey in the same number of days it takes a normal person to travel *down* the Colorado river. Obstacles such as the Hoover Dam, dangerous rapids, and steep canyons all were conquered because he planned beforehand how to get around them.

A person who has no goals becomes the victim of whatever comes along. Why do so many people become addicted to drugs? They have not made plans for a purpose or goal in life. Others become trapped by the cults, get in trouble with the law, or end up on welfare. What a waste! They are like the man the Beatles sang about years ago ... "He's a real nowhere man, sitting in his nowhere land, making all his nowhere plans for nobody, doesn't have a point of view, knows not where he's going to..."

What about you? Are you a "nowhere man?" Who are you in God's overall plan? Where are you going? Do you know what God's purpose and plan is for your life? Are you following that plan?

St. Paul said:

> I therefore so run, not as uncertainly; so fight I, not as one that beateth the air: But I keep my body under control, and bring it into subjection: lest by any means, when I have preached to others, I myself should be a castaway.
>
> *−1 Corinthians 9:26-27*

> I press toward the mark of the high calling of God in Christ Jesus.
>
> *−Philippians 3:14*

Too many people end up on the scrap heap of life because they set no goals. Sigmund Freud promoted the erroneous theory that goals were dangerous because there is a chance of failing to reach them. He reasoned that if a failure occurred, your self respect would be damaged and you would become neurotic. What craziness! The irony of that situation is that Freud himself set goals. He had aspirations. He wrote books and reports, and had goals that propagated his teachings back at the turn of the century.

Freud was wrong. Failure to set goals is far worse than setting a goal and not reaching it. For example, it is better for a student to set the goal of an "A" average and get a "B" average, than it is for him to set no goals and get a "C" average. Having no goals is tragic.

Scripture Meditations

> Philippians 3:14
>
> 1 Corinthians 9:26-27
>
> Proverbs 2:6-9
>
> Proverbs 3:5-7

Thought Provokers

What is the definition of a goal?

If a person has no goals, what is the result?

Why is scheduling your time important if you want to achieve your goal?

Chapter 29

In What Areas Of Your Life Should You Set Goals?

I believe that everyone should sit down and prayerfully set specific goals in five areas of his life:

1. Spiritual

(Examples)

a. Read 2 chapters from the Bible each day.

b. Spend 45 minutes in prayer each day.

c. Read a good Christian book every month.

d. Share my faith with seven people every week.

2. Personal

(Examples)

a. Lose 20 pounds by March 1 — 1200 calories a day.

b. Get a haircut every four weeks.

c. Jog 1 mile each day at 6:00 a.m.

d. School: achieve an "A" average this term

3. Family

(Examples)

a. Read 3 books each year on family living.

b. Spend one full day a week with family.

c. Take wife to dinner once a week.

4. Ministry

(Examples)

a. Write a Christian book by December 30.

b. Set up new training classes by September.

c. Train 50 ministers a year.

d. Make at least 10 home calls per week.

e. Church growth: 30% this year

5. Professional

(Examples)

a. Listen to one tape a day about my occupation.

b. Get 15 new customers each week.

c. Call on 25 prospects per week.

d. Financial goals.

Satan is aware of the value of organization. That is why he will do whatever he can to hinder you from setting goals and being organized. He will try to get you to put it off until a time that is "more convenient" or tell you that it's going to be too much trouble. He will tell you that you do not have what it takes.

If you allow the devil to convince you of that, it is likely that you will never be very successful or effective. Consider carefully these five areas of your life: spiritual, personal, family, ministry, and professional; prayerfully setting concrete goals in each area. Otherwise, you may fall into the 95% category of people who merely drift along, never arriving anywhere.

If you refuse to accept defeat, and wholeheartedly determine to get your goals down on paper, you will automatically increase your chances of being on target. The best way to hit the bull's eye is to aim at the center of the target. Do it today!

Scripture Meditations

Psalm 127:1-5

Psalm 128:1-6

Thought Provokers

List three traps which Satan uses to keep you from setting goals:

Make out a goal work sheet:

Spiritual Goals   Date:

Personal Goals   Date:

Family Goals   Date:

Ministry Goals   Date:

Professional Goals   Date:

Chapter 30

Goal Setting Rules

Setting goals requires that you follow certain fundamental rules. Like anything else in life, there is a right way, and a wrong way to set a goal.

A goal must be specific.

Unlike a vision, which is the entire picture, a goal gets down to the specifics. A vision is the *what,* the goal is the *how to* for accomplishment. A goal cannot be a vague generality such as "to be used of God" or "to have a ministry." Instead, a goal sounds like this: "I want to write a Christian book on tithing," or "I am going to take linguistic courses so I can work in Bible translation."

If all you have is a vague vision, begin right now to seek the Lord diligently in prayer and meditation and find your calling.

For instance, I am called to be a pastor-teacher in the body of Christ. That is my vision, my dream, my general walk in life. However, I have set specific goals within that framework. My goals are to teach lessons, write sermons, magazine articles, pamphlets and books, and to minister to others. Writing a book is not my calling. That is one of my specific goals within my calling.

God created us as goal-seeking creatures. It is almost impossible for us to go after a formless, obscure, uncertain target. It is relatively easy for us to move toward a definite, predetermined, visualized goal. That's why goals must be determined, specific, and concrete.

You should prayerfully set your own goals.

Generally speaking, *you* should be the one who determines your long term and short range goals in your life. Of course, depending upon your circumstances, these goals should be within the boundaries set by your employer. However, you are the one who will dictate what your specific aims will be.

Successful businessmen plan their day by setting priorities and objectives they want to accomplish. This gives them a schedule of events to follow, and keeps them from having interruptions.

A business woman told me that her boss sat down with her and helped her set some job-related goals. He did not do it for her, he just asked the proper questions, and she did it herself. As a result, she advanced from sixth place in sales the district to second place.

Goal setting could mean the difference between winning and losing; success and failure. Do not let someone else set your goals for you, do it yourself. Otherwise, you will lose your enthusiasm.

A goal should always take you closer to fulfilling your vision.

Do not squander your time and effort in areas in which you are not called. If you never plan to use chemistry in your life calling, do not set a goal of getting a degree in chemistry. You will be wasting your time and resources. Goals should always pull you closer to your God-given vision. If they do not, they are not God-inspired goals. Some students take subjects in college without considering what kind of work they want to do when they finish. That is a result of lack of a God-given vision. As a consequence, they find out that there are no jobs in that area, or that they have to move to another city, or they like studying the subject but hate it as a profession.

Since I am a pastor, it would be senseless for me to set an annual goal to read 52 unrelated books or novels. That would not help me, it would not help my ministry, and it would not help other people. Instead, I like to make the practice of taking out the junk. I eliminate the things in my life that are unrelated or harmful to my goals. My God-given call is too important for me to waste my time on junk that does not contribute to it.

Many ministers and professional people do not realize the consequences of wasting time on non-essentials; that's why they go backwards, and not forward. When setting your goals, be certain they will take you closer to accomplishing your overall purpose in life.

A goal should be written.

Writing down your goal helps you to formulate it and confirm it in your own mind. King David, when he designed the temple of the Lord, wrote it down, and was given understanding of all of the details of the plan.

1. The Lord was guiding David. To make your dreams, goals, and plans come true, you will need the guidance of the Lord just like David.

2. David understood the plan. It has been proven that if you can write something down, it shows that you have a pretty good understanding of it.

3. He wrote out the plans or the goals. If you do not understand your dream, putting it on paper in specific terms will help you gain the understanding necessary. By writing out your goal, idea, or plan, it will help you to crystallize your thinking, something that is of paramount importance.

4. David's plan was detailed. It was specific. The more details you include, the fewer mistakes are made during the project.

Out of the 5% of all people who have goals, only about 3% ever bother to write them down. Yet, statistics prove beyond question that the 3% who have written goals accomplish 50 to 100 times more during their lifetime than those who have goals, but never bother to write them down.

I hope that you see the value of this. When you put your goals in writing, you are not just thinking about them, you are actually visualizing them. If you can see your goal, it is easier to achieve your goal. Blindfolded target practice is very difficult.

Your goals should be challenging.

A challenge creates enthusiasm, a much needed ingredient for success. If you are an insurance salesperson, and last year you sold 375 policies, it would be no challenge for you to set a goal of 200 policies for next year. You know you can do it. There is no excitement or enthusiasm generated. If you challenge yourself to see 500 policies, that is an exciting commitment! It will get results.

Suppose you said, "I'm going to give up spinach for Lent! I don't like spinach anyway." What kind of accomplishment would that be? Instead, if you are dieting, eliminate the food that gives you the most problems.

Why are ministers content to settle for ministering to 100 people effectively when God's vision is for much more than that?

Can you imagine Jesus saying, "I will be satisfied if I can get just a 100 people saved and teach them the principles of the Kingdom?" Certainly not! Jesus challenged us to reach the entire world: *Every single human life.*

Don't be content to level off. Your ministry will die.

In Korea, Dr. David Yonggi Cho, pastor of the world's largest church, knows the importance of setting challenging goals. He started with a goal to reach 200 people with the gospel. Then after reaching it, he set a more challenging goal of 500, then 1000, then 5000, then 10,000, then 50,000 until today he has over 700,000 members in his church. God gave the results because this man dared to keep challenging himself with higher and higher goals. Do not set weak goals. To be affective, goals must be challenging!

Your goals should be realistic.

Do not start by setting a goal such as, "I am going to build a rocket and fly to the moon next week," especially if you do not work for NASA. Do not try to gain 50,000 new church members in a year if your church size is only 100 members now. Be realistic. Do not go ridiculously beyond your faith or God-given ability.

Set a challenging, but realistic goal. Break down your overall goal into a 10 year goal, 5 year goal, 2 year goal, 1 year goal, 6 month goal, 3 month goal, and so forth, until you have a goal for the day. Make your goals big, leaving room for God to work miracles, but do not bring reproach upon your faith by setting your goals way beyond what God is doing.

Dr. Cho did not set out with a goal of half a million members in one year. He started with a realistic goal that was challenging to him at the time.

Your goals should include a deadline.

Unless you set a target date for you to accomplish your goal, your goal will be more like a vague wish. "Well, I hope I can get this done someday." A bride will go crazy if she is planning a wedding without a set date. If you set a goal, but do not put a deadline on it, you are likely not to get it done at all. This creates frustration.

Deadlines provide a little bit of pressure for us to get busy and finish the task before us. Most of us work better under pressure. A deadline will keep you from napping. Remember, if you snooze, you lose.

Ask yourself what the best target date is for accomplishing each step of the project; then set realistic deadlines. A goal is not a goal unless it is assigned a deadline. Like the goal itself, deadlines should be realistic. A contractor makes his living by bidding a job, setting a deadline for its completion. If he is wrong in his estimate, he loses money. An inventory planner controls the production of a manufacturing company by watching the lead times on the parts he orders, and the production schedule. The more accurately he can predict the deadlines, the smoother the operation becomes. A late part can hold up the entire assembly line.

Suppose we set no deadlines. If an inventory planner says, "Oh well, we will begin the project sometime next week," or "I will order the part when I get around to it," what will happen? The operation would grind to a halt. Without deadlines, it's easy to put things off or wait until conditions are better. It is better to remember these universal laws:

1. Work expands to fill the time available for its completion. In other words, if you set an open-ended goal, your work will keep increasing to fill the time available for its completion. Unless there is a deadline, the goal cannot be accomplished. This is called Parkinson's Law.

2. If you wait for perfect conditions, you will never get anything done (Ecclesiastes 11:4 TLB). When a goal has no deadline, we have a tendency to wait for perfect conditions. For example, if I had no target date for the completion of this book, I would revise it, correct all the poor grammar in it, and change things around continuously. Every day,

I would think of something else to improve on in this book, an illustration, another chapter. I would never finish it if I waited until it was perfect.

Our church has certain goals that are set for every department. These goals are set by each department leader within the framework of our larger corporate goals. They are encouraged to find creative ways to reach these goals. Each one has a target date assigned to it, and progress is evaluated each month. This gives us a way to measure our progress.

Scripture Meditations

Ecclesiastes 11:4

1 Chronicles 28:19

2 Peter 1:4-10

Deuteronomy 11:18-25

Thought Provokers

List the seven rules of goal-setting:

1.

2.

3.

4.

5.

6.

7.

Why does it help to put your goals in writing?

Write down a goal you have that is challenging, yet realistic. Assign a deadline to it.

Completion date:

What are the two results of not setting a deadline?

Why are conditions never perfect?

Chapter 31

Understand Scheduling

God works by time schedules. He set a time schedule for his creation. He made everything in its proper sequence at the proper time. Suppose He created the fish before He created the sea or the birds before the atmosphere? Neither would have survived, would they?

Jesus Christ, our Messiah, came to earth right on God's schedule. He rode into Jerusalem on the colt of a donkey the exact day God said He would. God has a time schedule for the return of Jesus. By the signs all around us, we are getting close to the deadline.

God has a time schedule for *you*. I believe that because we are in Christ, God directs our lives according to a plan and purpose. He does everything according to schedule in His time.

Keep a daily schedule. A schedule is faith goals listed in order in a timetable. The daily schedule will list everything you are going to do in order of its importance. Set priorities in your schedule. A way to do this is to rank them on a scale of 1 to 10, accomplishing the most important and most difficult tasks when you are fresh.

Priorities are determined by the following factors:

1. Degree of difficulty of the task.

2. How critical the task is. ("I must have this ASAP.")

3. Length of time it will take to finish.

4. Appointments you have to keep.

A task may not be critical, but it may also be easy to do and take only five minutes. Therefore, it can be fit in between other tasks and receive a higher priority. A task may be needed by the end of the week, but it takes a whole day to do, and all of your days are filled up with appointments except for Thursday. So, you schedule your critical task for all day Thursday, which is in effect lower priority because it's the only time you can schedule it.

The better you can fill your schedule and manage your time, the more you will get done. It helps to have a daily calendar or Day-Timer, where you plan your schedule. You can also get pads of paper that have on it, "Things to do Today" numbering priorities down the side.

A schedule helps you to do first things first. It is a mistake to start building a house before you dig the basement. It makes no sense to have to redo things just because you leave out a step. Make out a master schedule for your life, your business, your ministry. It is important to get your goals in the proper order.

Scripture Meditations

> Genesis 1
>
> Ecclesiastes 3:1-11
>
> Mark 13:24-37
>
> Matthew 24:3-31

Thought Provokers

What is a schedule?

For the following page, set priorities for a Saturday work day.

Priority:	Time:	Task:
_____	_____	Do the dishes
_____	_____	Fix supper
_____	_____	Wash the car
_____	_____	Make the bed
_____	_____	Fix TV antenna
_____	_____	Read the Bible
_____	_____	Take a nap
_____	_____	Work on a book
_____	_____	Mow the lawn
_____	_____	Change the oil in the car
_____	_____	Get a haircut
_____	_____	Chase skunk out from under front porch

Get a separate sheet of paper and plan your next week. Separate each day into hours, and put down what you want to accomplish and when.

Chapter 32

Goal Setting: A Review

Here is a list of the common mistakes in goal setting. While reviewing these points, think of your goals and how you will try to avoid making these mistakes:

1. Setting goals too low. This leaves no room for miracles. Goals that are easily achieved cause you to lose your excitement and enthusiasm.

2. Setting goals too high. This will bring a feeling of discouragement and defeat. You will be tempted to quit altogether if you realize that your goal was not realistic.

3. Failure to understand that goals must continually be set higher. Goals are only temporary resting points. As you attain one goal, prayerfully establish a new one, just out of reach. Unless you continue to grow and expand, you will eventually level off and die.

How to set your goals and achieve them

1. See the overall picture —the dream — the vision. God has a general overall plan for your life. Find out what it is, and set your goals accordingly.

2. Prayerfully set a goal by faith.

3. Develop a plan for reaching the goal.

4. Build a team if necessary. Gather people around you who share your vision and are willing to help you.

5. Always move on your own initiative. Once God has given you a goal, do not wait for the right mood or feeling. Paul told Timothy to stir up his gift. People who wait for the right mood to pray usually do not pray. People who are not self-starters will never get their engines cranked over.

6. Move ahead with great perseverance. There will be obstacles to overcome, but you can do it with the help of our Lord Jesus Christ. Remember, He is always with you.

Four reasons why most people do not set goals

1. They do not know how.

2. They are too lazy; they do not want to take the trouble.

3. They do not have the faith that God will help them accomplish their goals.

4. They have set goals in the past on a long range basis and did not see immediate results. They become cynical.

Scripture Meditations

> 1 Corinthians 9:26
>
> Hebrews 11:1
>
> Mark 9:23
>
> 1 Chronicles 28:19

Thought Provokers

Can you think of a time when you set your goals too high? When?

What is your current primary goal?

What is the first step in successful goal setting?

"Make no little plans. There is nothing in little plans to stir men's blood. Make big plans. Once a big idea is recorded, it can never die."

— Daniel Burnham,
Chicago Planning Commission

Chapter 33

The Importance Of "Faith Movies"

Master level leaders plan their lives with these steps: defining their dream, establishing goals and deadlines, and possessing a "faith movie".

Christians should never try to accomplish great goals for God in the natural energy of the flesh. This is futile and frustrating. Those who try to do the work of God in the energy of the flesh will fall prey to stress and pressure.

God has not called us to overwork and stress. Some Christians act as if God hands out His righteousness only if they struggle for it. They do not seem to realize the tremendous price Jesus paid on the cross. He suffered for us so that our righteousness is His righteousness, and His righteousness is our righteousness.

In the sight of God, all of our striving and working to win the approval of God is nothing but filthy rags. Why do we try to substitute the work Jesus did on the cross with our work? Do we think His work was not good enough?

Yet, we toil away, as if we have to earn God's love. What a waste. God made the covenant with us, and we must accept it by faith. There is no more struggle, only trust.

Are you so foolish? After beginning in the Spirit, are you now trying to attain your goal through human effort?

— Galatians 3:3 NIV

Goals given to us by the Holy spirit cannot be accomplished in the energy of the flesh. The tasks God gives us are enormous, and when we look at them, we wonder how anyone can tackle them. Zerubbabel, the high priest, was faced with the task of rebuilding Jerusalem. God told him:

Not by might, nor by power, but by my Spirit, saith the Lord of Hosts.

— Zechariah 4:6

It is the Holy Spirit who gives us the energy, tools, and miracles needed to achieve the impossible.

After you set your goals, it is important to picture the end result of your goal with your eye of faith. Produce a "faith movie" of yourself successfully reaching your goals and deadlines. Picture Jesus being with you, helping you, guiding you. He said, "I'll never leave you nor forsake you. I'll be with you even until the end of the world."

Does placing a picture of a big, fat, enormous, overweight person on the refrigerator door help you to lose weight? I really don't think so. Looking at that fat person focuses our mind on the negative, and we automatically find ourselves hungry all the time because our system is trying to make us into what we see.

If you have a desire to lose 30 pounds of ugly fat, do not *see* yourself looking fatter. Picturing failure is not faith. If you ask for God's help, He will give you the vision of being slim and trim.

Some people think themselves into sickness. One woman was sure she was going to get cancer. That was her greatest fear. After going to the doctor for years, finding nothing, sure enough — she ended up with cancer!

We think in pictures. God can use this "picturing process" to formulate and shape your dreams. Once you are able to picture the end result of your goal, God will help you achieve it.

A Mighty Man of Valor

Gideon did not think much of himself. He was of the tribe of Manasseh, which was regarded with disdain in those days. He came from a poor family, and he deemed himself the least of his family. In Judges 6:12, God called him a *mighty man of valor*.

I can see Gideon saying, "Who, me?" God called it the way He saw it, not how Gideon thought. Once Gideon got the vision in his own mind, he *became* a mighty man of valor and led the children of Israel to victory.

Abraham's Children

Although he had no child, God showed Abraham the stars of heaven and promised him that his offspring would be as numerous. Although Abraham and Sarah were well advanced in age and beyond childbearing age, God's vision kept gong through the mind of Abraham. In his spirit, he would remember the words of the Lord. Then, the miracle happened. Sarah gave birth to Isaac, and eventually, Abraham became the father of many nations. That's a "faith movie" or "seeing with the eye of faith."

Ministering to Hundreds

When I first became a Christian, I started seeing myself as a preacher of the Word, ministering to hundreds of people. As I prayed, I would use this remarkable law of the Spirit. I remember practicing my sermons and picturing myself in the pulpit. I would even practice by preaching to squirrels! I went over every detail in my mind and could literally feel myself being used of God as a pastor.

Without any human effort, pushing, or scheming for an opportunity, I soon found myself doing the very things I had seen in my "faith movie." The pastor of one of the largest churches in the community asked me to come and preach. In a matter of months, I was preaching to hundreds. The image I had in my mind had come true.

Other preachers testify to the same thing. One would preach from a closed down hot dog stand as a boy. Nobody was there, but he still would preach with all his heart. His grandmother once told him "someday you will be preaching to thousands of people." He meditated on these words and saw them in a "faith movie" coming true. Today he is not only preaching to thousands, but millions!

Cancer Healed!

Harry was diagnosed as having terminal cancer and sent home to die. One day he received a Christian magazine in the mail that had an article in it about a woman who had been healed by the power of faith in God. This got Harry to thinking, "Is there really power in faith?" Soon, he began to pray with childlike faith. As a result of his prayers, God gave him a heaven-sent idea. "Begin to see with your eye of faith healthy white cells within you marching down your body and doing battle with the unhealthy cells." So Harry did this several times a day, praying, believing, and seeing his faith movie. Suddenly, one day he noticed he was hungry, whereas before he had no appetite at all. He began to eat well and started felling better. After many weeks, his astonished doctor told Harry that the disease symptoms were gone. Today, Harry is a healthy man!

A Barren Woman Made Fruitful

The prophet Elisha told a barren woman that she would be embracing a child next year about that time. Why do you think that he used the word embracing instead of just telling her that she was going to have a baby? Perhaps it was to help her visualize something specific, like actually holding the child rather than just having a baby. No doubt this was difficult for her to believe. Elisha's words made it much easier, because she could then get a picture of it in her own mind. Sure enough, Elisha's prophecy came true.

> And he said, About this season, according to the time of life, thou shalt embrace a son. And she said, Nay my lord, thou man of God, do not lie unto thine handmaid. And the woman conceived, and bare a son at that season that Elisha had said unto her, according to the time of life.

> — 2 Kings 4:16-17

The Fields Are White Already To Harvest

Jesus used the illustration of the wheat field to help the disciples visualize every human being as a stalk of wheat ready to receive the gospel. He said:

> *Lift up your eyes and look on the fields; for they are white already to harvest.*

> *— John 4:35*

That is His commission to use: let's not wait to reap the harvest until conditions are right, go after it now!

Every time you go by a wheat field, remember what Jesus said. Picture yourself as a great soul winner, leading people to Jesus Christ as easily as harvesting wheat. Do not see yourself leading only one or two to God (as important as that is) but imagine yourself as a farmer harvesting a whole field; leading hundreds, yes thousands to Christ. Think BIG. Produce BIG "faith movies". There is great power available to those who learn this principle.

Scripture Meditations

Galatians 3:3

Zechariah 4:6

Judges 6:12

Judges 6:34-35

2 Kings 4:16-17

John 4:35

Thought Provokers

How do "faith movies" help you accomplish your faith goals?

Write out the script for a faith movie that applies to your own life.

Chapter 34

Negative Visualization

Your imagination can be used either for good or for bad. Worry, negative talk, and a poor attitude feed a negative self image, damaging your faith. What you say is often what you become. That is why the Psalmist said:

Let the words of my mouth, and the meditation of my heart be acceptable in thy sight, O Lord, my strength and my redeemer.

— Psalm 19:14

Listen to the words that come out of your mouth. They are a reflection of the image you have of yourself. Negativism is a disease of the heart that destroys a person's effectiveness in leadership and ministry. Have you ever heard anyone say this? "I just can't get started today." "I don't know why I always keep making the same dumb mistakes over and over." "I can't possibly do that!" "Well, I'll be damned!" "I don't have enough experience." "All of the good jobs have been taken." "Well, I'll be a blue-nosed gopher!"

See what I mean about negative images? What kind of pictures do you see when you hear these statements? It is a wonder that anything is accomplished at all with the negative images people have of themselves. God is ready and willing to grant us what we see by faith. He wants us to have a positive image of ourselves so that He can bless us. If we harbor negative thoughts and ideas, we allow the devil to destroy us according to the thoughts and images we have of ourselves.

Worry Is A Negative Faith Movie

Worry is a negative "faith movie." It sees the bad up ahead, real or imagined. This type of imagination is not pleasing to God because it displays a distrust in His promises.

An exiled president of a South American country constantly worried about being killed. It was his biggest fear. He would visualize himself being assassinated. In his mind, he would go over and over every detail. Finally, it happened. What he greatly feared had come upon him. The headlines read, "Exiled President Shot."

The devil knows the power of "faith movies." He tries to get this law to work against people. That's why some forms of media can be so destructive: pornography, health scares, bad news, recession, depression, wars, and rumors of wars. Whatever you picture in your mind is what you eventually become. That is why we must filter out negative input from the TV and newspaper. Negative input will cripple your creative abilities and pollute your mind. If the devil can accomplish that, you will fall short of reaching your God-given goals.

It's simple. If you contemplate failure, you will most likely get failure. If you see yourself falling short of your goal, you probably will. If you picture yourself reaching your goals, with God helping you, regardless of the number of problems and setbacks that are involved, *you will achieve success.*

After setting your goals, picture them already in existence. Do it *now!* Establish a faith image in your mind of your accomplished goal. Real faith "calls those things which be not as though they were," (Romans 4:17).

Don't Get Discouraged

If you do not know exactly how you are going to achieve your goal, do not be discouraged! Simply pray and picture the end results. God will give you heaven-sent ideas when you need them. Sometimes, He purposely withholds the "how to" information to make sure that you continue to be humble and remain close to His perfect will.

A good horse will respond to the leading of the rider with just a little tug on the bridle. Often, a horse will have blinders on his eyes so that he is totally dependent upon the rider's direction. Otherwise, he may see something at the side of the road that distracts him and makes him jump. That is the way we should respond to our Lord's direction. "Lord, help us to keep our blinders on to the things of this world, and keep us from the worry and tension of the things around us. Instead, we completely trust in You and respond to the gentle tug of Your leading." If we do not worry, God will send people or even angels to help us achieve our goals. We must see the end result and have a faith image of where the Lord wants us to go.

Men and women who have achieved great things for God all have something in common — they are people of vision. On the other hand, check the accomplishments of their critics. Quite often, they have made very little progress of any lasting value to the kingdom of God, and the success they have achieved is usually at the expense of others.

PICTURE THIS:	NOT THIS:
1. Success!	Failure
2. Reaching your goal!	Falling short
3. The right doors opening!	Brick wall
4. Results!	Frustration
5. Health!	Sickness
6. Prosperity!	Poverty

| 7. God's Word! | Profanity |
| 8. Well being! | Fear |

Scripture Meditations

Psalms 19:14

Romans 4:17

James 3:1-12

Proverbs 23:17

Mark 7:20-23

Philippians 4:7-9

Ephesians 5:1-7

Thought Provokers

What can you do to improve the image you have of yourself?

Gives examples of negative words you should avoid using.

God changed Jacob's name from Jacob, which means "supplanter", to Israel, which means "Prince of God". What kind of names could you give other people that would encourage them to bear fruit for God?

Why is worry negative visualization?

Chapter 35

Dealing With Stress And Pressure

Have you ever bent a piece of stiff wire back and forth until the wire began to heat up where you were bending it? Eventually, it snaps in two. Have you ever taken a balloon in your hands and squeezed? After squeezing harder and harder, it eventually bursts. That is what stress and pressure can do to you. It can wear you down to the point where you could eventually crack up or break down. What can you do to stave off these deadly diseases in your ministry?

One of the best ways to avoid stress is to be aware of the causes of stress. If you can identify the areas that are giving you trouble, you can then concentrate on them.

There are three major areas that cause stress:

1. Life change.

2. Work related.

3. Environmental.

A life change stress occurs when a physical change occurs within your life style. The degree of stress involved can vary widely. The most stressful change of all is the death of a spouse. Then come divorce, marital separation, death of a close family member, personal injury or illness, new marriage, all the way down to such relatively modest changes such as getting ready for a vacation, getting a traffic ticket, or changing a job. This is why the elderly often die soon after their mate's death. The burden of losing their mate can be too much for them. Some never are able to make the adjustment.

Work related stress factors can include role ambiguity, role conflict, role overload, time frustrations, lack of pastoral care, lack of chances to get away, relocation to a new area or job, career uncertainty, and loneliness.

Your environment can also cause stress. Noise, pollution, crime, racial tensions, conflict with neighbors or coworkers, and breakdown of the equipment are all environmental stress factors.

Signs of Stress

1. Forgetfulness
2. Trouble seeing alternative actions
3. Temper flare-ups
4. Inability to change harmful patterns
5. Body seems to need more and more sleep
6. Frequent illness (colds, etc.)

//////// *DANGER ZONE* ////////

7. Having trouble keeping pace
8. Feelings of failure
9. Reduced sense of reward
10. Sense of helplessness
11. Cynicism and negativism

According to Dr. William Menninger, stress is perhaps the leading culprit in:

1. Psychosomatic illnesses
2. Headaches
3. Tension
4. Skin disease
5. High blood pressure
6. Heart disease
7. Some allergies

Every year over 500 million dollars worth of tranquilizers are used to help cope with the stresses of living. Tests have indicated that each person has only a certain measure of tolerance to negative stress, and the effect is cumulative.

In any ministry, you can expect a certain amount of stress and pressure. Satan will see to that. In every situation, God has given us the necessary means in which we can circumvent that stress.

> *There hath no temptation taken you but such as is common to man: but God is faithful, who will not suffer you to be tempted above that ye are able, but will with the temptation also make a way to escape, that ye may be able to bear it.*
>
> *— 1 Corinthians 10:13*

In this verse, the word temptation also means trials and tests. God always has a way out, no matter how bad the situation becomes. If we trust God to be faithful to us, He will provide the answer.

Scripture Meditations

Numbers 11:10-17

Ephesians 6:12

2 Corinthians 1:8

1 Corinthians 10:13

Thought Provokers

Give an example of each of the three different types of stress you have experienced:

Life change

Work related

Environmental

What signs of stress have you experienced?

What steps have you taken to manage stress?

"There's plenty of room at the top, but there's no room to sit down."

— Helen Downey

Chapter 36

Avoiding Frustrations In Time Management

Time frustrations are a big cause of stress. Someone has said that 90% of all of the world's problems are caused by unreasonable expectations. If you are managing a major business or ministry, you may find all of your time eaten up by interruptions, meetings, disorganization, and personal habits.

It is important to schedule your time. If you are constantly interrupted by the telephone, by people who drop into your office, or "emergencies," you will never get anything done, and you'll end up with crisis management. To avoid "fire fighting," make sure that whatever is top priority is always given your immediate attention.

Meetings are often a waste of time, and increase stress and frustration. They are also costly. Suppose you have fifteen people in a meeting for three hours. If each person's time is worth $15 per hour, that meeting would cost you $675! For that reason, you should keep meetings short and to the point. Plan an agenda, set objectives, control people from hogging the floor and rambling on, then make decisions. Use a meeting only to set direction and clarify issues, make them infrequent, and do not try to solve problems in them. Instead, attack problems using only two or three people. If there are more than that involved, you will be wasting somebody's time.

Disorganization is another cause of time management stress. If you do not plan, or your priorities are fuzzy, or your information is confused, or your personal life is disorganized, what happens? You become frustrated.

Personal habits like procrastination will cause stress. It is so easy to put things off, and so difficult to catch up with them later. Another personal habit that catches up with us is trying to do too much. We tend to think that we are the only ones who can do the project right, and we try to do it all ourselves. Learn to avoid burnout by using the people around you to help. When swamped with too much to do, delegate.

In Numbers 11:10-17, Moses was trying to meet the needs of all of the children of Israel, and was so frustrated he wanted to die! How did Moses cope with the impossible task of having to meet the needs of too many people? He delegated his authority by assigning leaders to share his ministry. He broke the job down into micro-segments. He formed cell groups.

Such a plan of attack works well today. It is impossible to manage the task of meeting the needs of so many people by doing it yourself. If we look at the enormous task of winning the lost, feeding the hungry, and ministering to the sick on a world-wide basis, we are overwhelmed by the immensity of the problems.

If the task is broken down into small pieces, and everyone is given a part to do, the job gets done.

Each person has the same amount of time, 24 hours, available for him to use in his day. Even if you were the President of the United States, you would still have the same 24 hours. How does the President get his job done? By delegating his authority and assigning tasks to others, handling only the big problems his subordinates cannot handle.

Scripture Meditations

Numbers 11:10-17

Proverbs 13:22

Proverbs 22:3

Proverbs 22:29

Ecclesiastes 11:6

Thought Provokers

What is one way you can better manage your time?

Think of a way you can expand your ministry by delegation.

What do you expect to accomplish when you have a meeting?

Chapter 37

Are You A "Type A" Personality?

Hard driving competitive-type personalities often are victims of stress. These people are known as Type A personalities. Type A personalities are achievement-oriented. This is good, but on the flipside of this good quality, there is a special caution. Type A's seem to possess a greater risk of developing heart disease if they do not learn to creatively relieve the stresses of being an achiever.

You can find out if you are a Type A personality by taking this simple test. See where you fit in by checking these different characteristics.

Type A: Must finish something once it's started.

Type B: Can leave things unfinished.

Type A: Never late.

Type B: Calm and unhurried.

Type A: Highly competitive.

Type B: Not Competitive.

Type A: Nods, interrupts, finishes sentences for others.

Type B: Listens well, lets others finish speaking.

Type A: Always in a hurry.

Type B: Never in a hurry, even when pressured.

Type A: Uneasy when waiting.

Type B: Able to wait calmly.

Type A: Always going full speed ahead.

Type B: Easygoing.

Type A: Tries to do more than one thing at a time, thinks ahead.

Type B: Takes one thing at a time.

Type A: Vigorous, forceful speech.

Type B: Slow, deliberate speech.

Type A: Wants recognition by others for job well done.

Type B: Does not have to please others, works for himself.

Type A: Fast doing things.

Type B: Slow doing things.

Type A: Hard driving.

Type B: Easygoing.

Type A: Hides feelings.

Type B: Expresses feelings openly.

Type A: Few interests outside work.

Type B: Has large number of interests.

Type A: Ambitious, wants quick promotions.

Type B: Satisfied with job.

Type A: Often sets own deadlines.

Type B: Never sets own deadlines.

Type A: Always feels responsible.

Type B: Feels limited responsibility.

Type A: Always measures his performance by numbers.

Type B: Never judges things in terms of numbers.

Type A: Takes work very seriously. Works weekends, brings work home.

Type B: Casual about work.

Type A: Very careful about details.

Type B: Not very precise.

Type A personalities, though they are achievement-oriented, may run a greater risk of heart disease if the frantic activity is not controlled. It is generally healthier for a person to have a mixture of Type A and B behavior.

In themselves, Type A characteristics are not wrong. In fact, many of them are keys to success. However, it is when they are taken to extremes that they cause problems.

Did you find out whether or not you are a Type A? If you are, do not be distressed about it! There are many practical things you can do to help control your stress.

Scripture Meditations

Matthew 6:25-34

Luke 12:16-21

Haggai 1:6

Proverbs 17:28

Psalms 37:1-11

Thought Provokers

Why do you think a Type A personality is prone to heart disease?

What does a Type A person have that a Type B person lacks?

Not all of the Type A characteristics are bad. List the ones you think are positive, and how they should be controlled to prevent burnout.

Chapter 38

How To Prevent Leadership Stress

Anyone can become "burned out" due to pressure. Therefore, once we recognize the signs of stress filtering into our lives, we should take steps to prevent an overload. The stress that an average pastor bears would bring most people to their knees. That is why a congregation should be keenly aware of the time a minister spends in meeting the needs of the people. Most people do not realize that the pastor is on call 24 hours a day, 7 days a week. That is why it is important for him to take extended periods of time off.

No pastor should work more than 50 to 55 hours a week. Some authorities recommend that a minister should take weekly breaks, a long weekend every quarter, and a yearly break of at least a month. They also recommend a sabbatical every six to eight years.

Eight Ways a Leader Can Revitalize His Ministry

1. Find fresh spiritual disciplines such as new ways of praying.

2. Take time off to renew, reeducate, and recharge mental and spiritual resources.

3. **Establish support networks with fellow leaders.** Attend prayer meetings, and fellowship with people who give personal and spiritual support.

4. **Enrich life at home.** Take full advantage of time together or take marriage enrichment seminars.

5. Get regular exercise.

6. Face fears by confronting them and casting off the burdens.

7. **Practice self-assessment.** Some leaders never take the time to figure out what is happening to them, or they do not try to assess how to improve things.

8. **Laughter!** Your body will not let you laugh and develop an ulcer at the same time. Laughter has tremendous healing power.

These practical tips will also work for anyone who is a businessman or factory worker. Whatever your job, it's possible to become burned out due to stress. Some stress, of course, is good. It causes us to achieve. But, negative stress can bring on the symptoms of burnout.

With the right amount of tension, a violin string produces music. With too much tension, it breaks!

Many people attempt to do too many things at the same time. If a woman has three children still in diapers, teaches Sunday School, helps in the nursery, sings in the choir, and works outside of the home, she is a perfect candidate for burnout. She should instead focus on the one ministry God lays on her heart. It is probable that she cannot advance beyond superficial or second level leadership in any ministry until she cuts out everything except what God has called her to do. Once she does that, she will find that her stress and burnout will leave!

Five Ways to Attack a Brick Wall

1. Attack the obstacle.

2. Withdraw and quit.

3. Attack someone close.

4. Attack yourself.

-OR-

5. Look to God.

179

When people come up against a brick wall, they deal with it in five different ways. Some attack the brick wall, trying to bulldoze through the problem in their own natural energy. Others give up and withdraw. Some blame others for the problem and take it out on them. Still others end up blaming themselves. These are all poor ways of handling an obstacle.

We must remember that the author of confusion is the devil, and that God is the only one able to remove these obstacles. When we look to God for the answer, mountains will move out of the way. We must not think that we can solve our own problems and beat the devil in our own natural energy. We must not give up or blame others or ourselves. Once we see God's perspective on the problem, and that He has a way to handle it, we are on our way to having it solved.

Four Steps Toward Handling Your Stress

1. **Get alone.**

2. **Get a delegate.**

3. **Seek God.**

4. **Then, get back to work.**

Burnout can be prevented by applying these principles. Scheduling time away from your normal activities is a good start. Find someone to take over and help, then go into your prayer closet and seek God. After you are refreshed, then get back to work. You will find you will have accomplished more.

Scripture Meditations

> 1 Thessalonians 3:1-4
>
> 1 Kings 19:1-18
>
> Proverbs 17:22
>
> Proverbs 15:13

Thought Provokers

Can you think of another way you could help your pastor revitalize his ministry?

How can you revitalize your ministry or business, and prevent burnout?

How can delegation expand your ministry?

"Leadership: the art of getting someone else to do something you want done because he wants to do it."

— *Dwight D. Eisenhower*

Chapter 39

You Need To Educate And Delegate

Why is it that some ministries grow and others do not? One of the reasons churches and ministries do not grow is because of failure to educate and delegate. The Church as a whole seems to have lost sight of its main goal — to make disciples of men. If you put money and man hours into a manufacturing plant, but get nothing out the end of the assembly line, you are wasting resources. Likewise, if a church is putting money and man

Success   Failure   Success

hours into programs but the end result is no growth or discipleship, that church is failing in its mission.

The Church's Main Goal

The main thrust of the church is to build disciples for Christ. Within that main thrust is the threefold mission:

1. Worship

2. Evangelism

3. Building of the saints through training

For some people, discipleship is a nasty word. To them, it brings to mind regimentation and stiff indoctrination. To others, it means authoritarian leadership dictating people's lives. That is not what discipleship means.

Instead, a church that teaches and practices discipleship brings its members to the point where they are all moving ahead in one direction, and everything is done in decency and in order. This can only come through education and training.

Share Your Ministry

The reason we educate others is to train them to share the ministry of the church. One of the reasons a church does not grow is because the pastor tries to do it all himself. Most often, such a church will reach a size of 100 to 150, then level off and die.

The next leveling off point seems to be somewhere around 250 or 300. Many pastors will change churches because of burnout several times, each crisis point occurring when the congregation gets to be about 300. Until a pastor is willing to delegate his ministry to others, the church will rarely grow beyond that point.

Some churches function as a "processing mill," shuffling people in the front door, registering decisions for Christ, only to find them filtering out the back door after a few months. We had that problem until I discovered these principles. One year, we registered 200 decisions for Christ, but only grew by 12 people! The church became a revolving door; in one side and out the other.

Why didn't people stay? I discovered that it was because they needed to be grounded in the Word of God and plugged in the ministry. Churches that do not educate and delegate do not grow.

Two Missionaries

Two of our missionaries set out to evangelize two different countries. One missionary held big crusades outside the city, and thousands came to receive Christ. The other held small meetings, but he spent the majority of his time training future pastors and teachers. Later on, these two countries fell into the hands of people hostile to Christianity.

Which missionary do you think had the most impact on their country? The church in the first country, under pressure, folded. Because they were without training, the converts ended up reverting back to their old ways. It was the second missionary, who trained leaders of cell groups, and shared his ministry with others whose work lasted and flourished. The church not only survived in that country, it thrived!

Training Brings Growth

As Jesus did with the disciples, we should train people a dozen at a time to share our ministry. One person trained is equal to a growth in the church of 12 to 15 people.

Let's imagine God for a minute having a big adoption agency. "Okay," He says to His angels, "I've got 500 people who are going to get born again. Where will they get the best care?" He looks down and sees a church, "Let's see . . . here's a place where they are already making room for thousands of souls, training and preparing people for the growth. Not only that, they have home cell groups where they can get one-on-one fellowship. Well, I guess they'll do best right here."

Home Cell Groups and Congregations

Our dream at Mount Hope Church, as it should be for every church, is to go into all the world and teach all nations the gospel, as Jesus Christ commanded us to do. The only way for that to work is to start at the basic unit, the home cell group. A cell group is a small group of people, from 2 to 25 people, who get together for a Bible study, fellowship, and training. It is in these small groups that real hands-on ministry can take place and needs can be met.

When a cell group gets to be about 20-25 people, it is time for it to multiply into two new groups of about a dozen each. When cell groups of similar interests get together in a gathering of 50-150 people, this is a congregation. Then, on Sunday morning, all of the congregations meet together in a praise gathering.

Each type of gathering has its own particular function in the body of Christ and meets different needs. Only when a church begins to function in this manner can it fulfill the commission Jesus gave us to reach the whole world for the Kingdom of God.

Some people like small churches. When you think about it, a small church is nothing but an overgrown cell group. We believe in small churches, too, but they should be within the corporate body of Christ. Some small churches behave like amoebas, floating about in the sea all by themselves. They never can become a body because they cannot multiply gracefully. Once a church gets to a certain size, a multiplication is inevitable, whether it is controlled or not. Cells need to divide to become organs, which then make up the entire body of Christ. Ironic, isn't it? In order for the body of Christ to multiply, it needs to divide!

Cell groups give quality time to ministry and provide a gathering place for people to take care of personal needs and training of disciples takes place. Once a group reaches the size of 20 to 25 people, it starts to defeat that purpose, since it is not possible for the leader to meet all the needs. If a group gets to be too large, separate the people into smaller groups of 8 to 10 people, and have them meet in separate rooms. Then needs can be met while a new leader is raised up for a brand new cell group.

The Pastor's Role

The Lord calls a pastor to have the overall vision for the church. He is the overseer. He delegates his authority and ministry to others to carry out. For example, I do not flow well in the counseling ministry. God has raised up an associate pastor to handle this in our church.

The Lord gave me a vision one day of a man who had various parts of his body missing. There was an elbow missing, an ear missing, part of his leg missing. I asked the Lord what this was. He said, "That's your ministry! You lack in many areas, so I have given you others to fill in where you lack."

One time, I got the shock of my life. I received a call from a man in the hospital who insisted that I come up and pray for his healing. I told him that we had healing teams that take care of this, men and women who flow in the anointing of healing. However, this man insisted that I come personally. Finally, I went and prayed for him. You want to know what happened? He died! I am quite sure if he had allowed the healing teams to come instead of me, he would be alive today. God has placed me in the role of a pastor-teacher, and has assigned other gifts to flow in other people in the church.

Know Your Anointing

A well-mobilized team of disciples will bring success to your ministry. Every person has an anointing which God has given him to flow in and minister to others. Each of us must discover and use the ministry and gifts God has equipped us with.

If the ear should say, because I am not the eye, I do not belong to the body, would it be therefore not part of the body?

— 1 Corinthians 12:16

What was the ear's problem? He did not know what he was! All he knew was that he was not an eye. So what happened? The body of Christ suffered because it had an ear that was not functioning. That is the state of the church if we do not function in our intended ministry. Not only are we frustrated, the whole church is hindered in achieving its goal.

How many "lame" or "blind" or "deaf" churches do we have because the people in them do not understand their function in the church, and do not flow in their God-given anointing? Pastors need to have the body of Christ flowing in the anointing of each of their particular ministries and gifts so that they fill in the missing chunks in their own ministry. How can we do that?

First of all, we must find our individual ministry and gifts. There are many different types of gifts: personality gifts, charismatic gifts, ministry gifts, supportive gifts. We must explore all of the possibilities. Next, we experiment. If we feel a gentle tug in a certain direction, we need to investigate it.

Once we launch out in a direction, it's time to examine ourselves especially in the area of motives. After we check this area out, we need to stand back and evaluate our effectiveness. Is what we are doing bearing fruit? Then, expect confirmation.

Remember the five E's:

1. Explore all possibilities.

2. Experiment with a gift.

3. Examine motives.

4. Evaluate effectiveness.

5. Expect confirmation.

Selecting the Right People for Delegation and Leadership Under Your Ministry

If you are placed in the position of selecting a delegate or a leader, you should use this checklist in evaluating his potential. If you are called to be a leader, look over this checklist to evaluate yourself.

1. They should be recruited by God, have a desire and willingness to serve. They should have proved themselves reliable. This shows up by their enthusiastic participation in projects and programs in harmony with the senior leader's vision. In our church, prayer meetings and interaction (cell) groups are the priorities. I look for leaders who support these ministries (Acts 6:1-8).

2. They must have a deep relationship with God, not just external (Acts 6:5).

3. They must have a positive, faith-filled attitude (Acts 6:8).

4. They must exercise self-discipline. Do they smoke? Are they grossly overweight? Do they gossip? Can they control their tongue (Titus 1:9-11)?

5. They are organized. Check their personal lives (Proverbs 18:9).

6. They must be able to lead, not just preside (1 Timothy 1:5-7).

7. They should possess the ability to inspire faith and growth (2 Timothy 2:1-2).

8. They should possess good communication ability. Are they interesting and simple? Do they communicate well (Titus 2:8-10)?

9. They must be open, genuine, flexible, moldable, not set in their ways (Galatians 3:1-5).

10. They must be able to cooperate with others, both those over them and those under them (1 Corinthians 1:10).

11. They should be proven faithful in smaller things (Matthew 25:15-30).

How about you? Are you the type of person your pastor would pick for a major project? If so, good for you! It will be only a matter of time until God honors and confirms your ministry. If not, *do not give up!* Just understand that God will take your willing heart and use it. The rest will come along as He deals with you. Remember that people can be greatly used by God even though they feel they lack certain credentials. What you feel you are lacking, God will make up for it.

Scripture Meditations

> Matthew 28:19
>
> Ephesians 4:11-12
>
> Luke 9
>
> Luke 10
>
> Acts 6:1
>
> Proverbs 25:19
>
> Proverbs 26:9
>
> Acts 13:44
>
> 2 Timothy 2:2

Thought Provokers

Why do you think that most churches never expand beyond 300 people?

What can a church do to prevent the revolving door syndrome?

List what you think your gifts are.

What are some of the steps you are taking to plug into the ministry and calling God has given you?

"Most great men and women are not perfectly rounded in their personalities, but are instead people whose one driving enthusiasm is so great it makes their faults seem insignificant."

— Charles Cerami

Chapter 40

Overcoming Obstacles

What do you think is one of the most prominent signs of a Spirit-filled life?

T R O U B L E!

Satan does not mess with lukewarm Christians a whole lot or people who are "wishy-washy" and double minded. They are not much of a threat to his dark kingdom. He will only give them an occasional poke, and dump them on the scrap heap when he is through with them. For anyone who is really advancing the cause of Christ, who is making great inroads into the kingdom of darkness, and who is on the front lines, doing warfare against Satan — expect *trouble, obstacles, trials, rejection, misunderstanding, and injustice.*

> *Wherefore take unto you the whole armor of God, that ye may be able to withstand in the evil day, and having done all, to stand. Stand therefore, having your loins girt about with truth, and having on the breastplate of righteousness.*
>
> *— Ephesians 6:13-14*

If an earthquake hits, only the strongest buildings are left standing. The person truly called of the Lord is the one left standing when others have fallen from frustrations, troubles, and discouragement. There is a shaking going on in this land. Our leaders, both spiritual and political, are being sifted, tried, tempted, and trapped. If we are going to be leaders, we should anticipate this shaking in our lives and be prepared to meet the obstacles Satan will present. Why does God allow these obstacles?

1. Problems always come before enlargement. A farmer has to cut down the forest, pull out the stumps, and clear all of the rocks out of the field before he can till it and make it usable for his crops. Then the weeds are overturned and the soil has to be plowed up and harrowed. Only then is the soil good enough for planting.

2. God hates pride. How can the will of God be accomplished when a pastor or missionary is promoting himself instead? Obstacles have a way of dealing with our pride.

3. Obstacles separate hirelings from God's chosen leaders. The average stay of a pastor in a church is only about three years. Why is that? Most likely it is because they treat their ministry as a job, not a calling.

The only time you do not encounter obstacles is when you are not doing anything! If you do not intend to plant the field, you will never have to dig out rocks or weeds. Effective, successful leaders have three weapons they can use in their warfare against obstacles: strong Christ-centeredness, vision and direction, and a callousness to defeat. Remember, God is on our side. He works with us and helps us accomplish the impossible. Suppose we wanted to climb a mountain, but the mountain was only three feet tall. Where would the challenge be? A championship weight lifter does not get in shape by lifting feathers. He pumps iron! In the same way, obstacles build character by giving us spiritual exercise.

Obstacles keep us honest when we are trying to reach our goal. There are no short cuts around them. Instead we have to persevere through the obstacles to reach the goal. The end never justifies the means.

For example, Shadrach, Meschech, and Abednego went into the fiery furnace with the right attitude, in spite of how things looked. They knew God was able to deliver them, but even if He did not, they knew that they were not going to bow down to any golden idol.

In the Old Testament, God gave the children of Israel the Promised Land, but there still was a fight involved. They had to overcome the Canaanites.

God has given you a vision and a ministry. Are you ready to face obstacles? Do you expect God to simply hand you your dream? No, He does not do that. He expects you to dig in and work out these obstacles.

A farmer had a gigantic rock that kept him from plowing his field. After leaving it along for a long time, he finally decided to tackle the project and try to remove it. He got out all of his tools and his tractor, gathered several hired hands to help him, and began to dig it out the rock. Once he pried underneath it, he discovered that it was only a few inches thick and totally flat! He could move it with ease.

That's the way obstacles often appear to us. On the surface, they are big and tough to get around. Once we dig around them and expose them for what they really are, they are not so difficult after all. There is one word that will catapult you over every obstacle: *perseverance!*

Stick to it! Hang in there! God will give you the power.

Scripture Meditations

2 Corinthians 4:8-11

Ephesians 6:13-14

Psalms 138:7

2 Corinthians 4:16-18

Revelation 17:14

James 1:2-4

2 Corinthians 3:5

Psalms 4:1

Acts 4:18-32

Acts 5:12-16

Acts 13:44, 45, 49

Acts 6:1, 7-8

Acts 14:1-3

Luke 8:43-56

Thought Provokers

All of us have suffered from rejection at one time or another. Write down an example from your life, and how you handled it, or will handle it.

List three reasons why God allows obstacles in our lives.

What weapons do effective, successful leaders have in dealing with obstacles?

Chapter 41

Obstacles: A Stage Of Faith

God is preparing us for His eternal kingdom! What an exciting life it can be when we realize the potential of serving the Lord throughout eternity. A young artist, when he accepted the Lord Jesus, imagined what it would be like in heaven where he could spend a thousand years on a painting. The reward in heaven that will be waiting for us will be determined by our faithfulness here in this life. Our faithfulness will also be tested by our ability to overcome obstacles.

That is why it is such a shame that many people quit when they encounter an obstacle. Quitters never win. Winners never quit. Paul and Barnabus in Acts 12:24-25 had a mission to fulfill: to win the lost. In spite of obstacles, they did not quit until that mission was accomplished and the *Word of God grew and multiplied.*

In every worthwhile vision, you can expect to be kicked around. However, you can determine the direction of the kick. When you get the boot, make sure you have moved in a forward direction. An obstacle is only a stage of faith. As you learn to overcome one obstacle, you will be ready to face more exciting challenges with stronger determination. Do not quit.

You have heard of Ronald Reagan, Abraham Lincoln, George Washington, Teddy Roosevelt, and Arthur J. Phlogiston, haven't you?

Arthur J. Phlogiston? Oh, he is the one who quit.

When someone gives up, it is a terrible waste of resources. Think of all of the projects you have laying around the house waiting to be finished. All those projects that you have given up on or have encountered obstacles and are just gathering dust in your basement. Have you given up on your goal? It is time to tackle that obstacle and continued on to complete your dream? There is no mountain that cannot be moved.

Scripture Meditations

Acts 12:24-25

Philippians 3:14

Psalms 3:6

Proverbs 22:13

Thought Provokers

What is it that could cause you to set aside your dream?

What will it take for you to get going and accomplish it?

Why does it take faith to overcome obstacles?

"Instead of worrying about what people say of you, why not spend your time trying to accomplish something they will admire."

— *Dale Carnegie*

Chapter 42

Different Types Of Obstacles You May Face

No doubt you are going to face obstacles. However, you need to eliminate the obstacles that are self-imposed. We have enough trouble in this world without creating more ourselves. What are some of these self-imposed obstacles?

1. Fear of problems (Psalm 118:6).

2. Fear of other people (Proverbs 29:25).

3. Fear of failing again (Isaiah 43:18-19).

4. Fear of imperfection (Ecclesiastes 11:4 TLB).

Obstacles like these set in only when we start believing the little lies the devil whispers in our ears. Why should we be afraid of any of these little things? We will always have problems that confront us, there will always be people to stand in the way, we may fail; and, without a doubt, we are imperfect, but why should that stop us before we even get started? If your goal is God-breathed, nothing can stop it, unless *you* stop. So, get started!

Once you get beyond the self-imposed obstacles, you will need to be aware of the other kinds of obstacles you may face, and how they will surface. A leader will always face problems with other people, more so than most people, because of their vulnerable position.

Carnality

Some of the most negative people are those who know a little bit of the Word of God. They are carnal because they do not meditate on it and apply it to their lives. They are often the ones who cause the most problems in a ministry.

Misunderstandings and Wrong Information

Often there will be misunderstandings that take place between two people. It is very easy for people to misread your motives for doing something. Sometimes, they will listen to you but will hear something totally different than what you said or meant. At other times, it is wrong information that causes the problem. This is why it is so important for Christians to depend and rely upon the voice of the Holy Spirit. The Holy Spirit never gives wrong information.

Different personality gifts can cause misunderstandings in the church. Typically, a person with the ministry gift of ruling or administration will not be gifted in the area of mercy. Where a "ruler" will tend to appear more callous in a situation that calls for judgment, the one gifted with "mercy" will call for forgiveness. That's why God has given different people different gifts, to create a balance.

Complaints

Listening to too many complaints can be an obstacle. We must be able to distinguish between a legitimate complaint and harassment. When a complaint is legitimate, it produces quality control and always takes you in a forward direction. **Legitimate:** "Pastor, there's a problem in the youth department where cliques are forming which exclude some of the kids. I suggest we break up these cliques and have the leaders divide the kids up into cell groups during the youth services." **Harassment:** "Pastor, I don't like the job the youth pastor is doing. The kids aren't getting ministered to, and it just seems like a social club." Legitimate complaints offer a *solution.*

Rumors

Rumors often damage ministries. If a malicious rumor surfaces, try to trace it to the source and expose it.

Criticism and Persecution

Criticism and persecution can be much more harmful than complaints. This type of obstacle is formed by a person who questions the motives of the leadership and tries to break down authority. Usually the people who do the most criticizing are the ones who are doing the least work. Persecution occurs when the person who criticizes is clearly in the wrong and has no recourse but to persist in his error by mocking and scoffing. If you are encountering such opposition to your ministry, you must really be dealing with one of the devil's sensitive spots. Do not let this kind of criticism bother you.

Financial Obstacles

One of the toughest obstacles for a ministry to get around is in the financial area. Nothing will ruin a ministry faster than having it go bankrupt. The best way to deal with this problem is *use God's principles!* There are no shortcuts around the seed principle. We cannot reap where we have not sown. We cannot build the kingdom of God using the world's financial system. Do not borrow from the world.

An Unsympathetic Mate

An unsympathetic mate can be a tremendous obstacle to a ministry. Two locomotives were hitched to a train and they built up a full head of steam. There was a tremendous grinding noise, sparks flew, smoke poured out, a lot of energy was expended, but they did not get anywhere. Then, they finally figured out that the locomotives were going in opposite directions. One engine was turned around and they were able to pull a heavy load together.

That's the way a marriage should be. Both need to be in agreement on a goal. If your mate is going in the opposite direction you are going, your ministry cannot be affective. What can you do? Sometimes the best thing to do is to be patient and wait. God is able to answer your prayers and deal with your mate. The worst thing to do is to take the matter in your own hands and create more smoke and sparks.

One pastor divorced his wife and married another because he thought she was hindering his ministry. He is now selling life insurance. His ministry? Failed. Down the tubes!

If your mate is contentious with your being in the ministry, start doing spiritual warfare on his or her behalf, binding the powers of darkness. Make sure you are offering up protection with a covering of prayer. If you have checked your spiritual direction and know what God has called you to do, He will take care of your mate's attitude.

Most of all, find ways to encourage and build up your mate. Make sure that your channels of communication are open. God will help you reach your goal, but do it on His terms.

Scripture Meditations

Psalm 118:6

Proverbs 29:25

Isaiah 43:18-19

Ecclesiastes 11:4

Romans 7:14-17

Romans 8:5-8

Thought Provokers

Can you think of any obstacles you are imposing upon yourself?

How can you deal with your self-imposed obstacle?

List the different types of obstacles that are caused by other people.

How can prayer help in dealing with an unsympathetic mate?

Chapter 43

Poor Methods Of Handling Obstacles

People react to obstacles in different ways, some positive, others negative. Here are some examples of harmful ways of handling obstacles:

1. Withdraw. Retreating does not make the problem go away; instead it gives ground to the devil.

2. Substitute goals. If your goal is to have a four bedroom house, do not let anyone talk you into a two bedroom house. If you are quail hunting, do not shoot at the rabbits; you will scare away all the quail. Maintain your priorities and do not be doubleminded.

3. Act defensive. Jesus did not do this. During His trial, He did not even answer His accusers. Another way to handle problems: do not take yourself too seriously. Allow a little humor to break the tension.

4. Become overbearing and difficult to get along with. Some people try to intimidate their way through a problem and force it, like the military commander who ordered: "All liberty will be canceled until morale improves."

5. Make excuses for the obstacles. Don't be like the man who said his mother-in-law drove him to drink. That's no excuse; his mother-in-law is not forcing the bottle in his mouth.

Instead of these negative ways of handling obstacles, try these helpful methods:

1. Double check your direction. Biblical calls are initiated by God, not man. Make sure you are not straying from the path to which God has called you.

2. Put your hands to the plow, fully committed to seeing the vision fulfilled. Focus on your strong points and build on them.

3. Remember, steady plodding and persistence bring prosperity. Consider the tortoise and the hare. The tortoise reached his goal because he was not sidetracked.

4. Remember that starting requires the most energy. Satellites take a lot of energy to get into orbit, but once they are in orbit, they do not take any energy at all, but inertia carries them.

5. Cast all of your cares upon Jesus. Remember that He loves you, and your goal is His goal. Do what you can, and let God do what you cannot.

Scripture Meditations

Mark 5

Acts 6:1-7

James 1:5-8

Matthew 7:7-11

Matthew 26:59-63

Thought Provokers

Are you responding to obstacles in a negative way? If so, how can you correct it?

What are some positive ways you can respond to an obstacle you are now facing?

"Where Example keeps pace with Authority, Power hardly fails to be obeyed."

— *William Penn*

Chapter 44

Authority, Rebellion, And Divine Discipline

This is a tough subject for most people to deal with, and especially for me. But, this is God's subject, and one that we need to know how to handle gracefully, according to Bible principles. This subject becomes all the more difficult to deal with since there are so many false and abusive teachings about it. It is clearly an area where we must tiptoe through the mine field and watch our step. We must not shirk our responsibility to proceed into this area when necessary.

God wants us to clean our own house. When He steps in, it usually involves major surgery, often to the point of amputation in order to save the body of Christ. If a little sore is neglected and becomes infected, it can threaten a life. It is better to deal with the problem when it is small, when it can easily be treated.

Authority is real. Rebellion is real. Divine discipline is real. No matter what the teachings have been concerning this subject, we should not abandon it. Church history is full of scandals, abuses, and misuses of God's Word that damage the cause of Christ tremendously. Therefore, if a brother strays, we need to know the Biblical way of dealing with him and restoring him.

Two Controversial Questions

1. **Does God have to allow some people to die before their time in order to prevent the hindrance of God's plans?**

2. **Does God allow Satan himself to bring serious complications into the life of a person who is hindering God's will?**

If you examine the Scriptures, you will find that both answers are "yes." 1 Corinthians 11:27-34 indicates that even in the act of communion we need to examine ourselves and discern the Lord's body lest we become weak and sickly or die. In 1 Corinthians 5:15, we read about a man delivered over to Satan for the destruction of the flesh, that his soul might be saved. This is serious business with God!

A person can be in only one of two camps: he can be under God's authority or he is in rebellion with Satan. Let us contrast these two principles.

God's Authority	*Satanic Rebellion*
Delegated as God chooses.	*Enlisted through deception.*
Produces good fruit.	*Produces no fruit or bad fruit.*
Order/organization.	*Confusion/disorder.*
Obedience to God's will.	*Following some other will.*
Sent by God and Church.	*Maverick: "Jesus and I have our own little thing going" attitude.*

Make sure that you do not confuse the two camps. Under either principle, there may be sacrifice, service, and cross-bearing. Both may look as if they are accomplishing something. God is more interested in obedience than activity or sacrifice (1 Samuel 15:22). It does not make any sense to go full speed ahead if you are going in the wrong direction.

True ministry is *sent* ministry. It does not make sense to launch out as a missionary to Africa if God has not called you there. Even if God has called you to Africa, there will be a time where He will prepare you for that ministry.

You do not send a two year old into a cage to tame lions. Many people have mistakenly gone into the ministry for the wrong reasons, or at the wrong time, and have failed because God had not released their ministry yet. What a waste! A true ministry will be sent of God, confirmed by the body of Christ, then move in God's timing. Pray that the Lord of the harvest will send laborers into the harvest. Jesus Himself was a sent one (John 3:17).

How do you know you are sent? Examine your motives. Make sure that you know beyond a shadow of a doubt that God has called you, and that you are ready for the service He wants you to perform. Has God prepared you? Do all of the checkpoints line up according to plan? If so, GO! Do not delay. If not, STOP and wait.

How do you know you have the authority to proceed? The best way to know is to have two or three leaders whom you respect verify your ministry, preferably without your solicitation. If God has spoken to you, He will speak to them, too.

Scripture Meditations:

1 Corinthians 5:1-5

1 Corinthians 11:27-34

John 3:17

2 Thessalonians 2:7

1 Timothy 1:18-20

Mark 9:37

Matthew 9:38

Acts 13:1-12

Thought Provokers

Have you ever had a circumstance where God dealt with you directly and disciplined you?

How did it help you grow?

Have you ever tried to launch out into a venture too soon? What was the result?

Can you think of an incident in your church where God dealt with someone harshly? What was the result?

*"Authority without
wisdom is like a heavy
axe without an edge,
fitter to bruise
than polish."*

— Anne Bradstreet, c. 1620

Chapter 45

How Satan Challenges God's Authority

Satan is the originator of rebellion. Right from the beginning, he challenged God's authority and was cast from heaven. Then, he caused Adam and Eve to rebel against God in the Garden of Eden. The result was traumatic.

The fruit of rebellion is tragedy. The Scriptures are filled with examples of people who rebelled against God's chosen leaders and met with divine discipline and tragedy. Consider these examples:

Example:	Result:
Abiram, Dathan, and Korah showed disrespect for Moses (Numbers 16).	*The earth swallowed them.*
Miriam rebelled and challenged Moses (Numbers 12).	*She became leprous.*

Example:	Result:
Absalom rebelled against David (2 Samuel 13-18).	*He was killed in battle.*
Gehazi got greedy and disobeyed Elisha (2 Kings 5:20-27).	*He contracted leprosy.*
Judas rebelled against Jesus (Matthew 26).	*He hanged himself.*
Ananias and Sapphira tried to lie to the church (Acts 5).	*Both were struck dead.*
Herrod set himself up as God (Acts 12:20-25).	*He was eaten by worms.*
Hymenaeus and Alexander blasphemed (1 Timothy 1:20).	*They were delivered over to Satan.*

As you can see, God considers this a serious matter. God does not tolerate rebellion, especially against His chosen servants. For rebellion is as the sin of witchcraft (1 Samuel 15:23). To speak evil of a man of God is like cursing him and trying to cast a spell upon him like a witch. Don't ever end up with such a spirit. God will not tolerate it.

In Acts 13, Paul, who was the sent one, encountered Elymas, the sorcerer, who stood against him. Paul, filled with the Holy Ghost, laid down these charges against him and told him he was full of subtlety (like poison which you cannot see), full of mischief (recklessness, not understanding authority), a child of the devil, an enemy of righteousness, and perverting the right ways of the Lord.

He then pronounced divine judgment (divine discipline) upon this false prophet and told him he would be struck blind. When that happened, it produced a redemptive result. The deputy of that country became a believer!

That is always the goal of divine discipline. It is redemptive in nature.

Scripture Meditations

Acts 13:1-12

Numbers 16

Numbers 12

2 Samuel 13-18

2 Kings 5:20-27

Matthew 26

Acts 12:20-25

1 Timothy 1:20

Acts 5:1-16

Thought Provokers

What is the result of speaking against a man of God?

Although Saul tried to kill David, David never spoke against Saul. Why?

Why is rebellion like the sin of witchcraft?

What is the result in the church after divine discipline has been issued (Acts 5:12-16)?

Chapter 46

Leaders Must Exhibit Unity In An Imperfect Age

Ministers who are truly sent by God have enough to think about without other Christians causing them trouble. Since none of us are perfect, it is highly probable that someday there will be something that a pastor might say which may offend you or he could be totally wrong on an issue. *Do not let Satan use you to divide the body of Christ!*

Christians who should know better have been the source of persecution for major ministries. God does not want that!

Because we are imperfect, there will always be disagreement on minor issues. We must be tolerant of each other's viewpoint, and allow for a certain amount of diversity. What do you think caused Judas to start off onto the path of rebellion against Jesus? When the woman poured the precious ointment on Jesus, Judas thought it was a "waste." Through that mistaken thought, Satan convinced Judas that Jesus was nobody special.

All it takes is one little misunderstanding or one little contrary thought to cause a major problem. That's what happened to Judas; it happens to many Christians. Satan picks them off, and uses them to confuse the body of Christ.

The Parable of the Tools

Mr. Hammer was presiding at a meeting of the tools. Brother Screwdriver complained, "Brother Hammer must go because he is always making noise, always knocking." Hammer responded, "Brother Screwdriver has to go because he has to be turned around all the time to get him to do his job." Someone else said, "Brother Plane has to go. He always wants to just touch the surface. He never goes deep." Plane added, "Brother Sandpaper has to go then because he is always rubbing people the wrong way." Sandpaper spoke up, "Then Brother Saw must go because he is always cutting things up and leaving sawdust all over the place."

Just then, the Carpenter of Nazareth spoke. "I need all of you. We have a job for each of you to do. Put yourselves in my hand. Let me use you." Hammer said, "Here am I, Lord, use me." Screwdriver said, "Here am I, Lord, use me." Plane said, "Here am I, Lord, use me." Sandpaper said, "Here am I, Lord, use me." Saw said, "Here am I, Lord, use me." So when each gave himself to the Carpenter, together they built a church for preaching the Gospel, a bridge of understanding, and a house for a Christian family. That is what happens when the tools are in the Carpenter's hands and are used for the purpose for which they were made. (Written by Jess Moody)

All of us are different, come from different backgrounds, and see things differently. If we were omnipotent, and knew all things, perhaps we would then have the right to complain and criticize. However, we are not, so the best thing to do is to give the man of God the benefit of the doubt.

The four Gospels, Matthew, Mark, Luke, and John were written by four different men. Their personality shows through in their writing, and each presents a slightly different perspective on the life of Christ. That does not mean that they do not agree.

God does not want any Christian causing trouble for any of God's anointed ministers. We must have unity of faith and unity of purpose. A house divided cannot stand. That is why we screen our leaders at our church. If we have a leader on our staff who does not understand our threefold mission and goals, and instead is seeking after another goal, he will cause trouble for the church. The Scriptures warn us, "Touch not mine anointed and do my prophets no harm," (1 Chronicles 16:22, Psalms 105:5).

Why do people rebel? It is because Satan deceives them. He creates misunderstandings, tells lies, starts rumors, and first thing you know, there is trouble and rebellion. What if you find out that you are following a false leader? What do you do then?

1. Confront him personally. If the problems are major, he will be accursed (Galatians 1:8, 2 John 9-11). If minor, it will work out.

2. If you can't work it out, leave quietly.

3. If the person is morally corrupt, go to him one on one first, then take another with you, then take it before the church.

In conclusion, make sure that if there are differences of opinion, misunderstandings and problems, use the direction of the Holy Ghost. Make sure that the ministry is sent, and that the end result is redemptive in nature.

Scripture Meditations

Ephesians 4:11-12

1 Chronicles 16:22

Psalms 105:5

Matthew 18

Galatians 1:8

2 John 9-11

Thought Provokers

How can you tell the difference between a false prophet and a minister who is sent by the Holy Spirit?

What is the scriptural method of dealing with a leader who is in error?

How can we prevent disunity in the body of Christ?

"Character is Power."

— *Booker T. Washington*

Chapter 47

Understanding Spiritual Authority

No doubt only a fool stands shaking his fist in the path of a freight train roaring toward him on the tracks. When God has a divine purpose He wants implemented, you'd better not get in the way. If you get in the way when He comes down to do a work, He can be a God of severity.

We as pacesetting leaders are enlisted to do battle and warfare for the souls of men. Satan has illegal possession of the world, and our job is to wrestle territory from him. Jesus holds the title deed; we are to put Satan under arrest and evict him. We must understand the authority God has delegated to us. First of all, remember, those who went without being *sent* were likely to be *rent*. If you launch out where God has not called you, you are in rebellion.

"Oh Lord, bless this little work that I have chosen to do. I have made it just for you. Doesn't it look nice?" Who was the first to try this approach? It was Cain. He thought his sacrifice was appropriate, after all he "worked so hard" on it. Then God showed him that he was in rebellion. Why was Abel's sacrifice accepted? Because he followed God's instructions.

Satan does not care about you preaching the Word if you are not submissive to God's authority. Why? Because we reproduce what we are. Satan laughs when a rebellious person preaches the Word. That's like the square peg in the round hole telling the round peg what to do. It is a discredit to the Word of God. If you are not where God wants you, you cannot bear good fruit. When God's people are submissive to God's authority, Satan trembles! That is why Satan always challenges spiritual authority. If he cannot undermine leadership from within, he will attempt to bring about outside pressure.

How do you know when you are sent by God? First of all, you need to understand what a wrong ministry is. God has placed every one of us in the body of Christ for a particular purpose. Not one of us is ignored. If we assume a position that is not our calling, not only are we neglecting what God has called us to, but we are likely keeping someone else from fulfilling his calling. It is a double sin!

Some of the characteristics of a person who is in the wrong place:

1. They responded to a need, not a call.

2. They are not committed long term.

3. They set the job up for themselves.

4. They maneuver and push their way into the job or ministry.

5. Their ministry does not produce lasting fruit.

6. Lack of preparation.

If you are sent by God, then these signs will follow:

1. Long term commitment.

2. Deep, long lasting desire for this ministry.

3. Preparation and training.

4. Submission to leadership of the church.

5. Opportunity for leadership delegated through church leadership.

6. Direction by the Holy Spirit.

7. Ministry produces fruit.

8. Satanic opposition.

Ministries sent by God are *powered* by God. Like the freight train rumbling down the tracks, they are virtually unstoppable. Why? Because God's authority rests upon them.

In Acts chapter 13, the church in Antioch ministered to the Lord and fasted. It was then that the Holy Ghost spoke to them and said, "Separate me Barnabas and Saul for the work whereunto I have called them." And when they had fasted and prayed and laid their hands on them, they sent them away.

Why was it that God was able to use Paul with such power? Because it was the Holy Ghost himself who sent him. It was not because Paul was perfect. It was the authority that was behind Paul that gave him power to perform miracles.

If a private puts on a general's uniform and struts around the base, he might fool a few people and get some respect, but eventually he will be caught for impersonating an officer. In himself, he has no authority. He could give orders, but nobody would have to obey.

How about you? Are you genuine, or are you an impostor? The seven sons of Sceva saw the disciples casting out demons and thought they would try it themselves.

> *And the evil spirit answered and said, Jesus I know, and Paul I know, but who are ye? And the man in whom the evil spirit was indwelling leaped upon them, and over came them, and prevailed against them, so that they fled out of the house naked and wounded.*

> *— Acts 19:14-15*

That is why a ministry must be backed by the authority of God. The evil spirit knew Jesus and Paul, but to the seven sons of Sceva said —"Who are these guys?"— and beat them. Why? God did not send them.

Is your name known in hell? If the seven sons of Sceva were sent by God, they would have had the authority to cast those evil spirits out of that man. Instead, they were just playing around with it, as if it were occult magic. When this event took place, great fear came upon the people, and they burned all of their magic books.

So, mightily grew the Word of God and prevailed.

— Acts 19:20

That is what will happen when true revival takes place, no worldly or unconverted person will dare to join the church, only sincere believers. We dare not minister outside of God's authority.

Scripture Meditations

Romans 11:22

Acts 5:1-14

2 Corinthians 10:3-6

Acts 13:1-12

1 Corinthians 5:5

Ephesians 6:12

Acts 19:13-20

Thought Provokers

Evaluate your place in the body of Christ. Are you trying to minister in an area where you were not sent?

Write down the ministry which God has laid upon your heart over the long term.

Have you prepared yourself for that ministry?

What additional things do you need to do?

Are you willing to wait for God's appointing?

What will bring God's authority to your ministry?

Chapter 48

Extra-Mile Leadership

What is the difference between an average leader and a supersuccessful one? It usually is not all that much. An average leader does only what he has to. A super-success adds just that little bit extra. He does it because he wants to do it.

David's men trained themselves to use both of their hands in hurling stones and shooting arrows out of a bow. Just this little bit of extra effort and training made them so strong that even the least was over a hundred men, and the greatest over a thousand men. If you set your mind to produce a little bit more quality than the next person, you are going to be put in charge of many!

Tom Landry of the Dallas Cowboys made this observation: "There's not that much difference between a pro and an All-Pro. It's not ability. The NFL is full of people with all kinds of capabilities. There are dozens of players that have the ability to be All-Pro. They only lack a little more drive, determination and application." If a professional baseball player bats .250, he will make about $50,000 a year. However, if he bats .333, he will make $500,000 or more! What is the difference? Only one extra hit every three games.

It's a sad commentary of our state of affairs, but it seems that mediocrity is what rules the work place today. If you observe a classroom full of students, it does not take very long for you to point out the ones who are satisfied to be "just average." Jesus called mediocrity being lukewarm. What did Jesus say he would do with you if you are lukewarm?

> *I know thy works, that thou art neither cold nor hot: I would thou wert cold or hot. So then because thou art lukewarm, and neither cold nor hot, I will spew thee out of my mouth.*
>
> *– Revelation 3:15-16*

Mediocrity makes you want to spit. If you go out to buy a new car, do you buy the one that has flaws in the paint job? No, an uneven paint job tells you that the person doing the job did not care about what he was doing. You begin to wonder what else is wrong with the car. It takes just one fly to spoil the soup.

Anyone can do just what he has to do. That is what most people do, just float along. There is not any shortage of opportunities for the person who consistently does more than he has to do, with a good attitude, and strives for *quality* in all that he does. Suppose your preacher walks up to the podium on Sunday morning and says, "I did not have much time to prepare today, so I'm going to speak just what comes off the top of my head." What will happen? People will think he does not care about them.

Do you want success in your ministry or business? Then strive for quality. When I lived in San Diego, there was an Italian restaurant that was in the heart of the worst part of town. It was always jam packed. The reason is because the owner would personally prepare your food, stop and chat with the customers, and make sure you had enough to eat. "You want-a more?" he would say in broken English. "I give-a you more!" Then he would heap another generous portion on your plate.

Years later, I visited San Diego again. All of the other restaurants I remembered in the downtown area had gone by the wayside and closed. All except that little Italian restaurant. It was still there. Why? Because the owner went the extra mile.

There is a formula for success that applies equally well to organizations or individuals: *Make yourself more useful!* Slothful people do not seek work, they try to evade it. They make up all sorts of excuses.

The slothful man saith, There is a lion without, I shall be slain in the streets.

— Proverbs 22:13

Lazy people have their lions. If they cannot find a real problem to worry about, they will make up one. In contrast, Paul used every opportunity to share, to work, and to spread the gospel. He was a human dynamo! If you become useless, no earthly employer would keep you. Instead, find extra ways your employer can employ you. Get extra training on your own time. Tackle projects that nobody else wants to do.

Compared to the benefits attached, the extra mile is a short mile. God himself went the extra mile when He sent Jesus. He did the best He could in bringing us salvation. He did not send an angel or use a human being. He sent us His only Son.

So, make a commitment. "From today on, Lord, I am now going to give You my very best service. I will not offer anything substandard. I will go the extra mile, and I will find ways to give extra quality to my work for You."

Scripture Meditations

1 Chronicles 12:2, 14

Matthew 5:41

1 Corinthians 9:23-27

Revelation 3:15-16

Thought Provokers

In your ministry, can you think of something a little bit extra that you can add to your service?

Think of a person you know who is a super-success. What extra-mile principles does he or she practice?

What are the characteristics of quality work?

"Preparation makes for leadership, and leadership is service to man."

— Dr. Douglas Southall Freeman

Chapter 49

A Leader Is A Teacher

There is a desperate need for sound teaching, and teachers who will go forth and instruct people in the Word of God!

Go ye therefore, and teach all nations, baptizing them in the name of the Father, and of the Son, and of the Holy Ghost. Teaching them to observe all things whatsoever I have commanded you: and lo, I am with you always, even unto the end of the world.

— Matthew 28:19-20

An individual in California, whom I will call Mr. Valentine, had a carpet cleaning business and was working hard on the job one sweltering day. Thirsty, he reached down and took a drink from his "water jug." It was a bottle of ammonia! He was not watching what he was doing, and the bottle was not clearly labeled. Therefore, he nearly lost his life. He had not intended to drink ammonia, but because of lack of proper information on the bottle, he did.

> *My people are destroyed for lack of knowledge.*

> *— Hosea 4:6*

Another individual, who I will call Mr. Hammond, contracted sugar diabetes and ended up with an amputated leg because he had a poor diet. Mr. Hammond lamented that he wished he had known that all of the cream puffs and sweets he ate would cause such a thing.

That's the reason why we need anointed teachers. Teaching helps prevent the common problems and accidents that disable the people of God. Who can teach? All may teach, even though not all have the gift of teaching or the office of a teacher. Everyone has the capacity to teach someone something.

> *Let the word of Christ dwell in you richly in all wisdom; teaching and admonishing one another in psalms and hymns and spiritual songs, singing with grace in your hearts to the Lord.*

> *— Colossians 3:16*

This is one way everyone can help. In a cell group, we build each other up with songs, poems, Bible study, and practical examples of Christian living. What is the objective of the teacher? It is to impart knowledge — which is a most important part of the learning process. Knowledge does not bring salvation, but without it we fall into error.

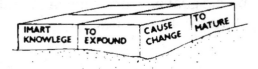

FOUNDATION OF TEACHING

We must come unto the knowledge of the truth (1 Timothy 2:4), increase in the knowledge of God (Colossians 1:10), and grow in grace and knowledge (2 Peter 1:2).

We need knowledge to explain and expound God's Word and principles in a practical way. Jesus did this on a variety of subjects. He handled practical matters, like dealing with money, and He used it to explain the kingdom of God. People were impressed and amazed at His teaching because He not only gave scriptural knowledge, but imparted understanding, and application for daily life situations.

Another reason for teaching is to cause a change in both attitudes and actions. Jesus inspired people to action. His illustration of the house built on the sand and the house built upon the rock got them to move from a state of listening to a state of practicing His teachings. Teaching brings Christians into a mature walk with Jesus. It helps people fit into God's program. Christian maturity should be the goal of every believer. We should be living stones, not dry bones.

Scripture Meditations

Matthew 28:19-20

Hebrews 5:12-14

Colossians 3:16

Hosea 4:6

1 Timothy 2:4

Colossians 1:10

2 Peter 1:2

1 Peter 2:2

Ephesians 4:13-16

Thought Provokers

Why do we need teachers?

How did Jesus give us an example as a teacher?

List some of the results of teaching.

Chapter 50

How To Teach For Results

"But, I can't get up in front of people! I'm not much of a speaker." How many times have you heard people say that?

When God called Moses, Moses told God to send somebody else, that he had a "slow tongue," (Exodus 4:10-17). How did God respond? He said, "Who made your mouth?" God sent him anyway. "But if you insist, I will have Aaron go along with you." *You can do it, too!*

> *Jesus said unto him, If thou canst believe, all things are possible to him that believeth.*
>
> *– Mark 9:23*

Unbelief is a thief. It robs us of our intended purpose in life. Do not think you are not able to do it! Jeremiah, when he was between 17 and 19 years old, was called by God and told: "Get up and dress and tell them whatever I tell you to say. Don't afraid of them or else I will make a fool of you in front of them."

How to Teach for Results

1. Be guided by God. Do not shoot from the hip, but endeavor to speak only the words of God. As Paul said:

> *For I determined not to know anything among you, save Jesus Christ, and him crucified.*
>
> *— 1 Corinthians 2:2*

Jesus said only the things which His Father in heaven commanded Him to say (John 12:49).

2. Always be helpful in your messages. Jesus made sure that all of his messages had practical truth and could be applied to daily situations. He did not expound on some vague metaphysical idea. Job complained to his "friends" that all of the advice they were giving him was useless. Do not become like one of Job's three "comforters," annoying people with all sorts of vain drivel. Make your teaching count. See to it that your sermons are strong and helpful, full of practical advice. Also, God does not call people to browbeat or discourage others. You will not find among the ministry gifts "church rebuker" or "church humbler."

3. Prepare. Preparation is part of our armor (Ephesians 6:15). A baseball coach once said that the will to win means nothing unless you have the will to prepare. Passover was a day totally spent in preparation. The more time you spend in prayer, thought, research, and study, the easier it is to teach, and the more effective it will be.

4. Know your subject! If you are a poor speaker, at least you will know your material. There is a radio preacher who has a heavy accent, but he is such a powerful teacher of the Word that his program is known and heard all over the world.

5. Pray, pray, pray, pray. Power and success come from God, not from our ability. We cannot do anything of lasting value by ourselves. Our only power and success come from God. Jesus instructed us to enter into our closet and pray secretly. Only then will the Lord reward us openly.

6. Be enthusiastic about your material (Romans 12:11). Never be lazy about your work, but serve the Lord enthusiastically.

7. Communicate in a way people can understand. If you have ever read some college textbooks, you would think there was a conspiracy to deliberately confuse the minds of people. Do not try to impress people with fourteen syllable words and deep theological and metaphysical ideas and thoughts. Instead, use illustrations and examples that are familiar to most people That is the approach Jesus used. He talked about farming, planting seeds, raising sheep, and weeds. In the King

James Version of the Bible, 84.4% of the words were one syllable, 14.2% were two syllables, and only 1.4% were more than two syllables. That is why the common people received Christ. He spoke directly to their need and understanding. When Paul preached on Mars Hill in Athens, he started right where the Greeks could understand: the Unknown God.

In Nehemiah 8:8-12, it was a time of great and joyful celebration because they could hear and understand the Word of God. The Wycliffe Bible Translators are dedicated to bringing the Bible to all nations on the earth in their own natural language. Just think of the problems you might have receiving Christ if the Bible was written only in Chinese or Russian. That's really what our work is all about, making the Scriptures and God's principles easier for others to understand. D.L. Moody once said that the successful preacher must preach plain. Remember the SOB principle:

S: Say it SIMPLE

O: Say it OFTEN

B: Make it BURN

You do not have to get it grammatically perfect, but your aim is to communicate truth and inspire action.

8. Speak with authority. When Jesus spoke, the people were astonished with His doctrine, for He taught them as One having authority, and not as the scribes (Matthew 7:28-29).

It is interesting that Jesus is said to have authority, and it was inferred that the scribes did not have authority. What was the difference? Jesus *knew* what He was talking about; the scribes must have hemmed and hawed. Don't be wishy-washy and talk all around a subject, never making a commitment. Keep your doubts to yourself, and preach on what you know to be the truth. Use support texts, quotes from people, testimonies and illustrations that you have verified as true yourself.

9. Use repetition. Repeating something over and over has a double impact. If you say something often enough, it will eventually sink in.

10. Don't be afraid. A song we sing has the message: Be bold! Be strong! For the Lord your God is with you! Why should you fear speaking and teaching? The truth is on your side. God has not given us the spirit of fear, but of power and of love and of a sound mind (2 Timothy 1:7).

11. Use personal illustrations and testimonies. Jesus did, Paul did, Peter did, Ezra did, and so did the prophets. Some colleges teach you never to say "I" in the pulpit. That's stupid! Personal examples bring life and fire to your message, since you are speaking directly from your heart and life experience.

12. Do not talk too much. Stephen, in Acts 7:1-60, gave a long drawn-out account of the history of the nation of Israel while he was standing before the scribes and Pharisees. When he was finally through, they ended up stoning him! Paul, in Acts 20:9 preached a long sermon, during which poor Eutychus dozed off and fell out of the loft to his death. Paul had to cut his sermon short in order to raise him from the dead.

These helpful hints should be kept in mind when you are organizing your teaching materials. God needs great teachers in His church. Perhaps He is calling *you* to be one of them.

Which Illustration Describes You?

Scripture Meditations

Exodus 4:15

Jeremiah 1:17 TLB

Mark 9:23

John 12:49

John 14:10

Acts 20:20

Job 27:12

Romans 12:7-8 TLB

Exodus 12:16

2 Corinthians 11:6

2 Corinthians 3:5

Matthew 6:6

Matthew 7:28-29

Nehemiah 8:8-12

Romans 12:11

Matthew 13:52

2 Peter 1:12-13

Ephesians 6:20

Acts 7:1-60

Acts 20:9

Thought Provokers

How can unbelief hinder a teacher?

How do you know you are speaking the Word of God and not some other word?

How can you make your messages more helpful?

Give an example of why you should prepare.

What is the difference between an enthusiastic and a dull teacher?

What is the difference between speaking with authority and wish-washy teaching?

Write a short personal illustration that communicates a spiritual truth.

Chapter 51

How To Organize Your Message

A teaching, sermon or message must be constructed in a logical manner. A haphazard or poorly thought out message always shows. A message is organized in the following manner.

1. **Introduction**

2. **Main Body which contains:**

    A. Main points.

    B. Scripture support.

    C. Illustrations (windows of a sermon).

3. **Conclusion**

4. **Call for action**

The Introduction is very important, since you must grab the attention of the listener right off the bat. Try to use a funny story, a shocker, or a stunt to start.

Examples: "You know, a lot of speakers start off with a story about what happened to them on the way to the meeting. I never do that. I never have, and I thought I never would ... until today!"

"Just the other day, witches dressed in their black robes had a seance across the street from our church, chanting and casting spells."

"You see this mousetrap? Now, what will happen if I sneak in here and touch this lever as lightly as I can..."

Did that get your attention? That's the purpose of the introduction. A good transition will lead you right into the main message.

The main body should be organized into main points. There are several ways you can do this:

1. 1-5 points

2. 1 point, 1 truth

   a. Bible illustrations

   b. Contemporary illustrations

   c. How to

3. Commentary (verse by verse)

4. Expository (take a scripture and expound upon it)

5. List (see 2 Peter 1 and Galatians 5:20-21)

6. Problem/solution

7. Extemporaneous

8. Combination of above

The Conclusion should have a good transition leading up to it, and it should summarize the main message. It is often helpful to tell them what you are planning to telling them, tell it to them, and then tell them what you told them.

Always end your messages on a positive note. Do not leave people hanging without a solution to a serious problem or build them up to let them down. A strong conclusion is the most important part of the message. When you finish, leave them with a call for action. Make sure they understand what they are being called to do, and tell them how. If it is a message of salvation, show them how they can receive Christ.

Some helpful hints: Notice what other preachers and teachers use in their sermons and take notes. Make an outline of their message.

Use these as resources:

1. Bible

2. Personal experience

3. Ask others

4. Books, magazines, tapes

5. Library

6. Bible helps, such as a concordance and/or Bible dictionary

7. References such as a dictionary or thesaurus

Teaching is a rewarding experience and good teachers are hard to find. Make up your mind to be one of them.

Scripture Meditations

2 Peter 1

Galatians 5:20-21

Thought Provokers

Draw up an outline for a teaching you would like to give.

Chapter 52

Causes Of Failure In Ministry

You need to be wary of the pitfalls that can occur when you are trusted with a ministry. In a church, God's judgment will start with the leadership first. God will not tolerate a leader who is straying off his path, since he has the potential of leading many people astray. If a leader starts out following the Word of God and teaches people the truth, then is confused by Satan and tempted into sin, the effect is like a string of dominoes. Many of the people who listened to his teachings will also fall into sin, or they will be disillusioned by his actions and blame God. There are many traps which Satan has laid for the leaders of God. Here's what they are and how to avoid them.

Carelessness With Morals

Samson's life was careless and immoral, even though he got his strength from the Lord. God used him for an occasion against the Philistines, but it could have turned out a whole lot better if he was not so careless with his passions. As a consequence, his eyes were put out, and he died during the destruction of his enemies. God forgave him, but he still had to pay the price.

Some Christians believe that all they have to do is ask forgiveness. It is true that God forgives, but the destruction that sin causes will still remain. If you drive a nail into a piece of wood, then pull it out, it'll leave a hole. Likewise, sin will leave its scars. Do not rationalize immoral activity. Do not think you do not have to make restitution.

There was a famous evangelist who held meetings all over the country caught flirting and sipping wine with a woman who was not his wife. Although he was confronted with his sin, he continued with it. What is he doing today? He is now lecturing for the American Atheists. His ministry is gone. His anointing is gone. Even his faith is gone.

Avoid the appearance of evil. A pastor was called by a woman who was having problems. She asked him to meet with her at a motel. Not thinking, he went over to talk with her, and as he was getting out of the car, one of his parishioners saw him with her. The rumors that spread from that encounter ruined his ministry, even though his intentions were honorable.

Wrong Marriage Partner

Nothing can hinder or help you more than your marriage partner. A spouse who flows in the Spirit of God and supports your ministry with encouragement is one of the secrets of success in the ministry. If a spouse hinders the work of the Lord and fails to give their mate encouragement in the ministry, it is as if his life in ministry is canceled. A pastor cannot be effective if his spouse disagrees with him all of the time.

The husband-wife relationship is vital to God's plan. God made it the center of His hopes for the human race. Just like the church, God designed the husband and wife to go in the same direction with the same purpose and goals. Should they oppose each other, it will hinder the work of the Lord. That does not mean that if you are married, you should throw out your mate for another. That is unscriptural. There is always a way for God to work in a marriage to make it effective in the ministry. When you are looking for your life partner, *pray, pray, pray*. Let God be your matchmaker, and then you will not be stuck with the wrong person.

Entering Into Leadership Too Soon

Often, young pastors who enter the ministry will run off when the pressures are too great. That is because they are not ready yet for the ministry. It takes time for a leader to season. If a leader is placed where he is not qualified, he will make irrational decisions and move out into directions God has not called him.

Let us review the qualifications for leadership:

1. Born again and Spirit filled.

2. Definite call to leadership; recruited by God.

3. Prepared.

4. Life measures up.

5. Ministry has been proved.

God will open the doors when a leader is ready to serve. I once sent out advertising brochures for my ministry, spending lots of money. What did I get from it? Not one response. Only when I turned it all over to God and forgot about doing it all in my own effort did I get an offer to preach.

Let Down in Prayer Life

Do not cease in praying. It is your responsibility to maintain your relationship with the Lord. As you pray, pray in secret and converse with the Lord. Some people lose their ministry by squandering their time watching the late show on TV instead of spending it listening to the Lord in early morning prayer.

Negativism

We are to take a stand against sin, disorder, and evil in this world, but we must do it all in a balance with the message of God's love. Denouncing evil continually without letting up for preaching the Good News focuses the attention on the negative things in the world, and may amplify their effect instead of getting rid of them. Fighting fire with fire usually is not effective. Instead, fight fire with water. Douse the flames of evil with God's love.

Slothful in Business

There is much more to ministry than preaching. Do not neglect the administration of your ministry. Details like taxes and records, weddings and funerals, or not getting tax exempt status can kill a ministry if they start to pile up and get behind. Pay attention to details. If you cannot, appoint an administrator who can. If a ton of bricks does not work, Satan will try to bury you with a ton of feathers. Little problems pile up and become big messes if you fail to deal with them one at a time.

Failing to Reach Young People

A church that consists mainly of older people has missed its ministry. Many churches in just a generation die off when the children grow up and leave the church. Why do the young people leave? It is because the older generation forms a clique within itself, or that the leadership fails to place a priority upon communicating to the young people.

Young people face problems today that the older generation never faced. Unless the older members deal with these problems and find solutions, they will lose their children.

Remember the two men in a truck who were lost in Nebraska because they used an outdated map? Churches who fail to reach young people are like them. They try to chart their course with methods that worked long ago, but may not necessarily work today. Learn to move along with what God is doing.

Wrong Methods of Money Raising

Some unscrupulous people who have claimed to be evangelists use methods such as "magic wallets," "holy water," "splinters of the cross," or "miracle wheat" to raise money. Such methods destroy the credibility of leadership.

Don't be like them. Instead, teach God's principles of tithing, sowing, and reaping. These principles of prosperity work! There is no need to resort to gimmicks. There should be no deceit in the use of money. Never say that money goes toward one purpose, and then use it for another.

Getting Sidetracked on a Doctrinal Hobby

Stick with the gospel, salvation, and Christ crucified. Nonessential doctrinal questions, such as "how many angels can dance on the head of a pin," are useless and waste time in your ministry. Remember the threefold mission of the church and stick to it.

Failure to Study

Some never rise above the stage of mediocrity because they neglect the reading of the Word. Always strive to better yourself and to improve upon your teaching and your messages. Never be satisfied to remain where you are in your knowledge.

Poor Counsel

There will always be people who are ready to give advice. Your job is to sort out the bad advice from the good. Every leader has his trusted counselors, people with whom he can trust his ideas without immediately passing judgment. A poor counselor frequently will be the one who offers unsolicited advice. If it is unsound, there will be a check in your spirit when you hear it. If someone gives you advice that you think is questionable, thoroughly check it out before accepting it. Sound advice will be confirmed by two or three people.

Temptation to Sectarianism

There is a tendency for people to gather together in their little cliques and stagnate in their little groups of "we four, no more." This is where splits in the church occur. Do not let your fellowship group become a secret little society club. Instead, spread yourself around, get to know others, and include new people. The body of Christ is a living organism, and death occurs if the members of the body become independent of each other and stop exchanging life among themselves.

Messiah Complex

Another pitfall is the tendency for leaders, when they are successful, to develop a "Messiah complex." John Alexander Dowie led a revival around the turn of the century and founded the city of Zion, Illinois. If you go there today, you will see the results: thriving, huge churches, and a clean little town with beautiful parks and all of its streets named after Biblical characters.

The original revival stopped when Dowie began to think he was Elijah. When that happened, he lost his ministry.

Making Excuses for Failure

Do not become defensive when one of your pet projects bombs. Instead, analyze the problem and discuss it with another leader. It is not your ministry; it is God's. God is the One rising up or shutting down ministries. A "successful failure" is where you learn from your mistakes and continue faithfully with the Lord. You may not have gotten the results you expected, but you have grown as a result.

Failure to Make Your Ministry Enjoyable

Enthusiasm shows up in ministries! If you do not enjoy yourself when you minister to others, it puts a damper on everything. God wants you to enjoy your ministry, and He wants other people to be enthusiastic about their walk with the Lord. How can you minister to people effectively, and preach the Word of God when you are down in the dumps? A crummy attitude can ruin a ministry like onions on a chocolate cake. Make one of your goals to create a lighthearted outlook and a merry spirit wherever you are. Find ways to build people up and compliment them. Show that you really like what you are doing.

Giving Up Too Quickly

Many ministers miss their calling that way. For some people all it takes is for Satan to give them one little swat and they run away with their tail between their legs, yelping. Persevere with your calling in the face of adversity when you encounter it. Thomas Edison tried over 1000 different filaments for his electric light bulb before he found one that would work. Do not give up!

Scripture Meditations

Hebrews 12:16-17 TLB

1 Corinthians 6:9-10

Leviticus 18:22-23

Romans 1:21-27

1 Thessalonians 5:22

2 Timothy 2:15

Thought Provokers

Perhaps you have seen someone's ministry fail. Give reasons why.

How can you avoid failure in your own personal ministry?

Give a biblical example of a failed ministry, and tell why.

Chapter 53

Essential Leadership Rules

Rule 1: Saturate your life with prayer and meditation.

This book of the law shall not depart out of thy mouth; but thou shalt meditate therein day and night, that thou mayest observe to do according to all that is written therein; for then thou shalt make thy way prosperous, and then thou shalt have good success. Have I not commanded thee? Be strong and of a good courage; be not afraid, neither be thou dismayed; for the Lord thy God is with thee whithersoever thou goest.

– Joshua 1:8-9

Be always in prayer seeking the face of God and asking him, "What is my next move, Lord?" When Moses received the ten commandments, spending time on Mt. Sinai with the Lord, his face shone after he came down from the mountain top. When we spend time with the Lord, it makes a difference in our lives, to the point where we stand out and shine. Praying in the Spirit helps, for we know not what to pray for, but the Spirit Himself intercedes for us. When you spend an hour in prayer, remember the 20/20/20 rule: Twenty minutes of praise in the Spirit, 20 minutes in petitions and listening to the Lord, and 20 more minutes of praise in the Spirit.

Rule 2: Remember, you cannot change people by direct pursuit.

Often a woman will marry a man in the hopes he will change his bad habits once he is married. That's foolishness. She cannot change him. Nagging someone does not help. It will turn him off and drive him away, no matter how tolerant he happens to be to such things. Nagging is not trust. You cannot change people: that is God's business. Accept the people with you in the ministry by God's grace. Be grateful and use them according to their talents. You will never receive a perfect worker. Be careful not to promote someone who has not done well in the past, hoping he will take off like a rocket. That's a lousy system of management.

Rule 3: Do not criticize a person for something he cannot change.

That's not only ineffective, it is cruel. Do not call someone "Schnoz" or "Fatso." Instead, be an encourager. Find something in that person that you like and build upon it. Do not alienate people with your words.

Rule 4: Be firm with strife causers.

A man that is a heretick after the first and second admonition reject; Knowing that he that is such is subverted, and sinneth, being condemned of himself.

— Titus 3:10-11

Unity is essential in the church. We must all be proceeding in the same direction, and we dare not be the one to stand in the way of the moving of the Holy Spirit. Follow the procedure laid down in Scripture for dealing with troublemakers in the church. Our usher staff is structured in such a way that if anyone begins to cause problems in a church service, they will deal with them in an unobtrusive way.

Rule 5: Remember: It's not how much you can do, but how well you can do it.

It's not "Am I doing everything I can?" but, "Am I doing the right things?" Remember the formula: creativity, integrity, quality. The reason God blesses some ministries and not others is due to these three things. Are you following the formula for success in your ministry?

Scripture Meditations

>Joshua 1:8-9
>
>2 Corinthians 3:18
>
>Titus 3:10
>
>Romans 16:17-18
>
>2 John 6-11

Thought Provokers

What are some ways you can improve your regular daily time of prayer with the Lord?

What is the best way to change people?

What are some of the things people cannot change?

What are the rules for dealing with a strife causer?

What is the threefold ministry?

Chapter 54

Conclusion

Leadership is a role. It is a role that must be filled with someone who has a heart for God, who is teachable, and who is servant hearted ... someone like you. I am honored that you have completed this book. I would be deeply honored if you would write to me. God has called me to encourage and motivate people who serve in leadership roles. I know it is tough at times being a leader, but the rewards are phenomenal! I believe *you* are going to continue being super successful for God. Always remember the words of Jesus:

Herein is my Father glorified, that ye bear much fruit; so shall ye be my disciples.

– John 15:8

You are a *PACESETTING LEADER!*

Bibliography

Bliss, Edwin C., *Getting Things Done*, Bantam Books, 1976.

Chafer, Lewis Sperry, *True Evangelism*, Zondervan, 1919.

Cho, Paul Y., *Successful Home Cell Groups*, Logos, 1981.

Cho, Paul Y., *Prayer: Key to Revivial,* Word Books, 1984.

Cho, Paul Y., *More Than Numbers,* Word Books, 1984.

Coleman, Robert E., *The Master Plan of Evangelism,* Spire Books, 1963.

Daniels, Peter J., *How to Reach Your Life Goals,* House of Tabor Books, Australia, 1985.

Dean, Dave, *Now is Your Time to Win,* Tyndale, 1983.

Douglas, Mack R., *How to Make a Habit of Succeeding,* Zondervan, 1966.

Dunkin, Steve, *Church Advertising,* Abingdon, 1982.

Eins, LeRoy, *The Lost Art of Disciple Making,* Zondervan, 1978.

Engstrom, Ted W., *Motivation to Last a Lifetime,* Daybreak Books, 1984.

Engstrom, Ted W., *Managing Your Time,* Zondervan, 1967.

Finney, Charles G., *How to Experience Revival,* Whitaker House, 1984.

Getz, Gene A., *Building a Good Reputation,* Victor Books, 1987.

Goodwin, Bennie E., II, *The Effective Leader,* Intervarsity Press, 1981.

Hocking, David L., *Be a Leader People Follow,* Regal Books, 1979.

Kuhne, Gary W., *The Dynamics of Personal Follow-Up,* Zondervan, 1976.

Kuhne, Gary W., *The Dynamics of Discipleship Training,* Zondervan, 1978.

Liardon, Roberts, *Breaking Controlling Powers,* Harrison House, 1988.

Lindsay, Gordon, *The Charismatic Ministry,* CFN, 1981.

Lindsay, Gordon, *Apostles, Prophets, and Governments,* CFN, 1975.

Mahoney, Ralph, *The Making of a Leader,* World Map Books, 1985.

Millard, Amos D., *Learning From the Apostles,* Gospel Publishing House, 1971.

Nee, Watchman, *The Normal Christian Worker,* Church Book Room, 1965.

Schaller, Lyle E., *Growing Plans,* Abingdon, 1983.

Shinn, George, *The Miracle of Motivation,* Tyndale, 1981.

Smith, Chuck, *The Reproducers,* Regal Books, 1972.

Sproul, R.C., *The Holiness of God,* Tyndale, 1985.

Sumrall, Lester, *Run With The Vision,* LeSea Publishing, 1986.

Towns, Elmer, *The Successful Sunday School and Teachers Guidebook,* Creation House 1976.

Wagner, C. Peter, *Your Church Can Grow,* Regal Books, 1976.

Ward, C.M., *Things I Didn't Learn in Bible School,* Logos, 1982.

Williams, Denny, *Leadership Life-Style,* Beacon Hill Press, 1983.

Wilson, Marlene, *How to Mobilize Church Volunteers,* Augsburg, 1983.

Yandian, Bob, *The Local Church,* Word of Faith, 1984.

Published by

DECAPOLIS
PUBLISHING

For a catalog of products, call:

**1-517-321-2780 or
1-800-888-7284**

For Your Successful Life

These video cassettes will give you successful principles to apply to
your whole life. Each a different topic, and each a fantastic teaching of
how living by God's Word can give you total success!

**THE PRESENCE
OF GOD**
Find out how you can have
a more dynamic relation-
ship with the Holy Spirit.

**FILLED WITH THE
HOLY SPIRIT**
You can rejoice and share
with others in this wonderful experience of God.

**HOW TO KNOW IF
YOU'RE GOING TO
HEAVEN**
You can be sure of your
eternal destination!

**WHAT TO DO WHEN
YOU'RE GOING
THROUGH HELL**
When you feel like you're
going through hell, you have a
choice to make.

A SPECIAL LADY
If you feel used and abused,
this video will show you
how you really are in the
eyes of Jesus. You are special!

**MIRACLE RESULTS
OF FASTING**
Fasting is your secret weapon
in spiritual warfare. Learn how
you'll benefit spiritually and
physically! Six video messages.

These and other videos
available from Dave Williams and:

DECAPOLIS
PUBLISHING

Expanding Your Faith

These exciting audio teaching series will help you to grow and mature in your walk with Christ. Get ready for amazing new adventures in faith!

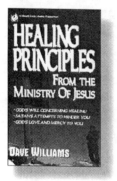

HEALING PRINCIPLES
Determine to walk in healing! "By HIS stripes, we are healed."

YOUR SPECTACULAR MIND
Identify wrong thinking and negative influences in your life.

FAITH, HOPE, & LOVE
Listen and let these three "most important things in life" change you.

THE BLESSING
Receive God's best for your life. He will pour out his blessing, an eternal act of love for you.

THE ANGELS SERIES
Angels are all around you waiting to carry out the will of God for your circumstances.

GOD IS CLOSER THAN YOU THINK
You can know that God is faithful. You can know He is never too far away.

These and other audio tapes available from Dave Williams and:

DECAPOLI
PUBLISHIN

Expanding Your Faith

These exciting audio teaching series will help you to grow and mature in your walk with Christ. Get ready for amazing new adventures in faith!

ACRES OF DIAMONDS
Find your own acres of "diamonds" right where you are.

FORGIVENESS
The miracle remedy for many of life's problems is found in this basic key for living.

UNTANGLING YOUR TROUBLES
You can be a "trouble untangler" with the help of Jesus!

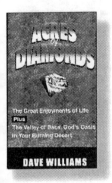

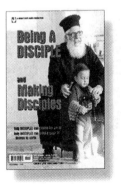

HOW TO BE A HIGH PERFORMANCE BELIEVER
Put in the nine spiritual additives to help run your race and get the prize!

BEING A DISCIPLE AND MAKING DISCIPLES
You can learn to be a "disciple maker" to almost anyone.

HOW TO HELP YOUR PASTOR & CHURCH SUCCEED
You can be an integral part of your church's & pastor's success.

These and other audio tapes available from Dave Williams and:

DECAPOLIS PUBLISHING

For Your Spiritual Growth

Here's the help you need for your spiritual journey. These books will encourage you, and give you guidance as you seek to draw close to Jesus and learn of Him. Prepare yourself for fantastic growth!

**BE A HIGH PER-
FORMANCE BELIEVER**
Pour in the nine spiritual addi-
tives for real power in your
Christian life.

**SECRET OF POWER
WITH GOD**
Tap into the real power with
God; the power of prayer. It
will change your life!

THE NEW LIFE . . .
You can get off to a great
start on your exciting life
with Jesus! Prepare for
something wonderful.

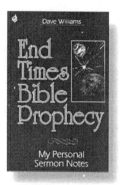

THE AIDS PLAGUE
Is there hope? Yes, but only
Jesus can bring a total and
lasting cure to AIDS.

**END TIMES BIBLE
PROPHECY**
Watch as events God spoke
about thousands of years
ago unfold to show us the
nearness of Christ's return.

**MIRACLE RESULTS
OF FASTING**
You can receive MIRACLE
benefits, spiritually and
physically, with this practical Christian discipline.

These and other books
available from Dave Williams and:

DECAPOLIS
PUBLISHING

For Your Spiritual Growth

Here's the help you need for your spiritual journey. These books will encourage you, and give you guidance as you seek to draw close to Jesus, and learn of Him. Prepare yourself for fantastic growth!

THE ART OF PACESETTING LEADERSHIP
Leaders are *made*, not born. You can become a successful leader with this proven leadership development course.

36 MINUTES WITH THE PASTOR
Join Dave Williams *this minute* for a daily dose of easy to understand devotions designed especially for you!

KNOW YOUR HEAVENLY FATHER
You can have a family relationship with your heavenly father. Learn how God cares for you.

SUPERNATURAL SOULWINNING
How will we reach our family, friends, and neighbors in this short time before Christ's return?

THE GRAND FINALE
What will happen in the days ahead just before Jesus' return? Will you be ready for the grand finale?

GENUINE PROSPERITY
Learn what it means to be truly prosperous! God gives us the power to get wealth!

These and other books available from Dave Williams and:

DECAPOLIS PUBLISHING

For Your Spiritual Growth

Here's the help you need for your spiritual journey. These books will encourage you, and give you guidance as you seek to draw close to Jesus, and learn of Him. Prepare yourself for fantastic growth!

SOMEBODY OUT THERE NEEDS YOU
Along with the gift of salvation comes the great privilege of spreading the gospel of Jesus Christ.

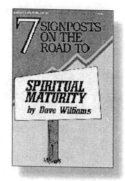

SEVEN SIGNPOSTS TO SPIRITUAL MATURITY
Examine your life to see where you are on the road to spiritual maturity.

THE PASTORS PAY
How much is your pastor worth? Who should set his pay? Discover the scriptural guidelines for paying your pastor.

THE DESIRES OF YOUR HEART
Yes, Jesus wants to give you the desires of your heart, and make them reality.

THE BEAUTY OF HOLINESS
Is holiness possible? Is it practical? How do you attain it? Find out how to pursue true holiness.

DECEPTION, DELUSION & DESTRUCTION
Recognize spiritual deception and unmask spiritual blindness.

These and other books available from Dave Williams and:

DECAPOLI
PUBLISHIN

Running Your Race

These simple but powerful audio cassettes will help give you the edge you need. Run the race to win!

LONELY IN THE MIDST OF A CROWD
Loneliness is a devastating disease. Learn how to trust and count on others to help.

SNAKE EGGS
Watch out for one of satan's deadliest traps — sexual sin. You can uncover his plot to put "snake eggs" in your mind!

HOW TO GET ANYTHING YOU WANT
You can learn the way to get anything you want from God!

A SPECIAL LADY
If you feel used and abused, find out how you really are in the eyes of Jesus. You are special!

ABC's OF A MIRACLE
You can learn the simple steps toward your miracle. Learn God's ABC's!

HOW TO KNOW IF YOU'RE GOING TO HEAVEN
You can be sure of your eternal destination!

These and other audio tapes available from Dave Williams and:

DECAPOLIS PUBLISHING